Praise for
The Google Infused Classroom

"When it comes to tech adoption I've always hesitated to lead with a tool, extension, or platform. When tech is seamlessly woven into what we do, when it's student selected and teacher supported, we attain powerful results. Our learners are more engaged, their learning is more vivid, meaningful, and complex, and my assessment of their understanding is more precise and accurate. *The Google Infused Classroom* is the first book I've discovered that supports deepening my understanding of this balance. Whether it's clarifying and sharpening my big ideas or narrowing my focus on how to maximize the potential of an extension, there's something in this amazing resource for everyone. *The Google Infused Classroom* will change your thinking and practice for the better!"

—TREVOR MCKENZIE, AUTHOR
OF *DIVE INTO INQUIRY*

"This book is essential for teachers to utilize as both a guide and a resource. Effectively implementing sound pedagogy with the right tools are the catalysts for inspirational learning opportunities. Tanya and Holly have provided the perfect roadmap for changing the traditional classroom to one that effectively uses technology to transform, enrich and amplify learning."

—KEN SHELTON, KEYNOTE SPEAKER

"*The Google Infused Classroom* is a valuable addition to any teacher's personal library. Tanya and Holly have brought together their years of experience implementing effective, sound educational technology in their own classrooms and packaged them into *The Google Infused Classroom*. You will find a plethora of practical ideas that can be seamlessly integrated into your classroom immediately, regardless of grade level. I love the fact that *The Google Infused Classroom* not only educates about the various tools, but focuses on best pedagogy as well. This book WILL disrupt traditional teaching methods, all the while focusing on how technology can AND will improve learning in your classroom. Enjoy the book. It's fantastic!"

—CRAIG BADURA, TECHNOLOGY COACH

"*The Google Infused Classroom* is a unique presentation of the marriage between good pedagogy and technology integration. It is beautifully laid out, with a design that makes it easy and fun to read. This guide can be used with any grade level and is great for teaching and learning in today's world!"

—SARAH THOMAS, EDUCATOR AND
FOUNDER OF EDUMATCH

"Holly and Tanya don't only talk about creative thinking in this book, the layout itself models innovation. Visually appealing and full of ideas, *Google Infused Classroom* is a friend to any teacher hoping to power up digital tools in her classroom!"

—Jennie Magiera, author of *Courageous Edventures*

"Tanya and Holly speak my language! *The Google Infused Classroom* is the perfect marriage of sound pedagogy and digital tools. This book is a must-have for any Google-using educator. Inside you will find practical ideas to perfectly infuse your class with quality strategies and the power of G Suite!"

—Kasey Bell, digital learning consultant at ShakeUpLearning.com

"What a phenomenally cool resource for teachers! Tanya and Holly do an amazing job of pushing thinking while prepping the reader to see paths for making all sorts of activities a reality for students. The apps and sites that teachers hear about are explained in the context of how to use them for specific learning outcomes along with information allowing the reader to choose among similar tools. I've been using technology for decades, and ideas in the book prompted new thoughts that excited me; this is a book for any teacher, regardless of accumulated experience, to make voice, choice, and audience vehicles for much better learning."

—Rushton Hurley, founder and executive director of NextVista.org

"*The Google Infused Classroom* is a must-have resource for all classrooms ready to take digital learning to the next level. Holly and Tanya have created a unique book full of practical ideas and classroom examples that amplify student learning while beautifully combining good thinking with technology integration."

—Lisa Highfill, co-author of *The HyperDoc Handbook*

"*This is THE book* for teachers using tech right now. Read it if you're past the "here's how this tech works" phase and want to implement it effectively. Read it if you're just starting with Google in the classroom and you want to do it right. Basically, read it! This book is the happy combination of sound pedagogy and powerful classroom tech that we need so much right now."

—Matt Miller, author of *Ditch That Textbook*

"*The Google Infused Classroom* is filled with important insights into the ways technology and pedagogy should work together to empower classrooms. Packed with examples of useful tools and transformational teaching strategies, this book should become part of every school's professional development library."

—Jason Markey, principal, East Leyden High School (Franklin Park, IL)

HOLLY CLARK & TANYA AVRITH

THE GOOGLE INFUSED CLASSROOM

A GUIDEBOOK to
MAKING THINKING VISIBLE
and AMPLIFYING STUDENT VOICE

The Google Infused Classroom
©2017 by Holly Clark and Tanya Avrith

These books are available at special discounts when purchased in quantity for use as premiums, promotions, fundraising and educational use.

For inquiries and details, contact the publisher: info@elevatebooksedu.com.

Published by ElevateBooksEdu

©2015 Google Inc. All rights reserved. Google and the Google Logo are registered trademarks of Google Inc.

Library of Congress Control Number: 2017941990
Paperback ISBN: 978-1-7336468-0-2
eBook ISBN: 978-1-7336468-1-9

THANK YOU...

From Holly Clark

To all my past students whose eyes lit up with excitement each time I tried something new, you each made me want to search out thoughtful and inventive ways of teaching. This book is dedicated to you.

To the parent who generously donated all the computers for my first 1:1 classroom in the year 2000. Without your philanthropy, I might have never made it down this path.

To Mike for making it possible for me to get this book done, and to Bella and Peyton who were always by my side during the process!

From Tanya Avrith

First and foremost, I would like to give thanks to my husband, Ronny, for his unyielding support and for encouraging me to pursue my passions. And to my children, Yael and Gabi, for inspiring me to always ask questions and never stop learning.

My parents, Sandra and Steven, instilled in me a love for learning and taught me the value of education.

This book is dedicated to all you amazing teachers who devote your lives to inspiring your students.

We also want to thank Rebecca Hare for her expert contributions in the design and development of this book.

CONTENTS

PEDAGOGY ◄ ••

THE TOOLS ◄·······································

Holly and Tanya have long been two educators whom I highly respect and have learned much from. They understand that the technology does not improve the learning or create the student engagement. Intentional lesson planning that considers how technology enhances and improves the learning is the key.

The Google Infused Classroom was written to help teachers look at the ways teachers can use Google and other online tools to help revolutionize the delivery model of instruction in a technology infused classroom. The book is based on the idea that by putting good pedagogy first, educators can use technology to powerfully impact student learning, ignite curiosity, and make the classroom changes our students deserve. The authors set us on a clear and easy path for understanding our learners, their needs, and how we can use these tools to meet them where they are and prepare them for a future that will involve little analog learning.

The authors provide a constructivist approach to learning. Using creation tools such as Google allows students to learn by doing, to take risks, and to take ownership of their learning. Both authors have a strong foundation in cognitive learning theory and use these ideas to help fuel the lessons in the book.

Holly and Tanya seek to inspire by using the framework of making student thinking visible. This framework allows teachers to better understand their learners—to know when they have learned and where they are in the growth process. Teachers can then use this important data adjust their teaching so each individual student's needs are met. The framework also gives teachers a place to begin using Google tools to amplify teaching and learning in the classroom—not just using them for traditional teaching tasks. The authors outline the tools and give instructions on how you can use them to accomplish good teaching strategies such as formative assessment and demonstrations of learning.

While tools are important, understanding the pedagogical ways we can use them to transform teaching is even more important, and this book lays out a path for allowing students to make meaning of content. As digital devices and technology tools become more prevalent class-rooms, we need more books like this that focus on the ways we can rethink instruction, looking at learning theory first and then at how we can use technology to support and amplify the learning experiences in our classrooms.

This book is a model for all to follow. It is time to disrupt classrooms and change the way we think about instruction, and this book will serve as a great starting point to help any teacher—regardless of their comfort level with technology. As you read it, you'll discover exciting ways to pri-oritize learning over technology and to use technology in a modern way, taking kids from a place of memorizing to a place of knowing.

How to Read This Book

When writing this book, we wanted to address the two common ways to think about transforming learning with technology: pedagogy and tools. We wanted to create an asset that would support and connect both ways of approaching technology integration. Maybe you want to find a better way to assess knowledge and understanding? Start with pedagogy. Or maybe you have heard about screencasting but don't know how to incorporate it into your instruction. Start with tools, page 113.

Starting with Pedagogy? Perfect!

The pedagogy section starts here and will give you some context for the learning theories that are the basis of the ideas presented in this book. We'll start with a focus on using technology to make student thinking and learning visible, giving every student a voice, and allowing them to share their work. From there, we'll jump into some basic pedagogical structures and provide some Google infusions that will enable you to remain faithful to pedagogy while amplifying your instruction with easy-to-use technology tools.

PEDAGOGY

PEDAGOGY

PED-UH-GOH-JEE

'\'PE-Də-,GŌ-JĒ

NOUN

The method and practice of teaching, especially as an academic subject or theoretical concept.

WHY GOOGLE?

Google is redefining what a learning space looks like, taking the traditional classroom and making it a place where we help our students visualize their thinking, give each and every one a voice, and allow them to share and publish their work.

This new learning space is a place where students gather feedback from their community—and the world—not always their teacher.

It is a place where they jump into a document and collaborate with peers—in their classroom, another city, or on another continent.

It is a virtual space where they could gather in a Hangout and help one another.

It is a space that amplifies teaching, where students interact with and learn from one another, where they reflect on concepts and ideas, and where they teach *us* what they know.

What is a Google Infusion?

A Google infusion is a fun way to partner the great tools available in the Google Ecosystem: Drive, Chrome apps and extensions, and Google Classroom—with another online tool to amplify teaching and learning in your classroom. Examples of simple infusions are using Google Classroom to pass out a Flipgrid or using the Chrome extension Talk and Comment in Google Docs. You may come up with your own infusions as you go through the book, and if you do, we would love to hear about them! We invite you to share your thinking and learning with the world—a practice that lies at the heart of this book. Be sure to the #infusedlearning hashtag when you share your ideas.

Disrupting
WHAT IT MEANS TO BE LITERATE

Remember when you had to pay to access Wi-Fi at places like Starbucks? Fortunately, those days are long gone! Businesses have realized that their customers value being connected, so they've made it easy for us to be online while shopping, eating, or waiting to pick up an order.

Our students also desire this connection. Each day, they are sharing pictures and posting status updates online—everywhere but in the classroom. Many of them, however, don't know how to share their ideas properly. Nor do they understand how to curate a powerful learning network online, cultivate an idea by finding and connecting with others who share their passions, or develop their ideas into something bigger. They haven't learned how to use the power of the Internet and connected learning because schools largely view technology and social media as distractions. Instead of having teachers guide and teach them how to use the incredible tools and information that are available, too many students are left to themselves to learn about being online, often in inappropriate ways.

Why don't schools allow students to connect online? In some cases, lack of funding for technology plays a role. More frequently, though, school bans on social media, Internet access, or technology in general is a product of fear, one found in our collective unconscious. Society periodically goes through massive shifts, where both information and how it's distributed changes. During the early stages of each of these shifts, people become uncomfortable. Throughout history, change has always brought about fears of how the new medium will affect society. We can go as far back as the invention of writing, which Socrates warned citizens against, fearing it would "create forgetfulness in the learners' souls, because they will not use their memories." Each technological advancement elicits new fears. With invention of the printing press, people feared that books would make them stupid because they would have no way of knowing the words' and claims' validity. Then the typewriter came along and people asked, "How will kids learn proper penmanship?" With the mobile phone, the worry was that they would cause a distraction in education. Technology and the use of social media in schools has now created another shift, many people fear (or at least are uncomfortable with) the ways society uses smartphones, mobile technology, and apps to connect and collaborate. These tools put so much of the learning of humankind at our fingertips, and we should consider them as extraordinary rather than dismiss them as distractions. Here's the good news about the naysayers of every shift: They almost always learn to be okay with the invention over time, and some even become proponents of the new technology once they get over their fears.

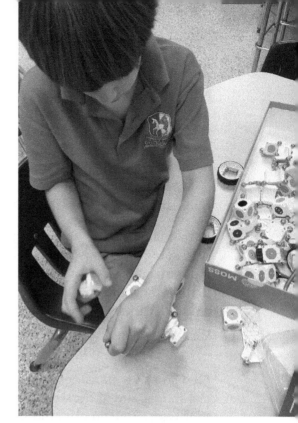

Redefining Literacy

In some popular science-fiction texts, authors present the ideas of a post-literate society in which multimedia technology has advanced to the point where we no longer communicate through reading and writing. With the advent of voice assistants, including Apple's Siri and Amazon's Alexa, it isn't hard to imagine a future that looks just like that. As we move into the twenty-first century, we need to teach our students to be "transliterate"—that is, fluent across all mediums of information, not just reading and writing.

If we're going to prepare our students for a technology-rich future, we must expand the definition of what it means to be literate. We need to create a disruptive shift in how we, as educators, define literacy. An important step toward accurately redefining literacy is to think of our students as participants in a global society, rather than simply as learners. After all, in their before- and after-school hours, students already connect in unprecedented ways. As connected global participants, they will need to develop crucial skills, including networked learning (an important part of the redefinition process) and the ability to understand and use different and new media. Before we can teach them how to develop and use these twenty-first-century skills, we must understand the process ourselves so that we can serve as ours students' Sherpas and help them explore these new forms of literacy.

Jump In

Most of us surf the Internet and post to Facebook, but those activities are not enough to understand the real power of learning one can experience online. If Facebook is your connection of choice, it is important to understand a few important facts: Facebook leans toward being more about social sharing than social learning, and the average Facebook user is 41.5 years old. What's more, although students are still using Facebook, they prefer Instagram, Snapchat, and YouTube.

With social media replacing newspapers and television as one of the first sources where people learn about the day's news and products, students need to be savvy about online information—how to find it, validate it, and then make sense of it. And if our students are to be successful in their future careers, they'll need to understand social media marketing, including tweets, retweets, hashtags, followers, and how to improve search engine optimization (SEO) rankings.

As disruptive, transliterate educators, we must learn how to speak social media and understand what it means to be connected learners so that we can guide our students. We must know and understand these new forms of information—how to use them correctly, what their nuances are, and how they are shaping our world. We must know how to curate information and crowdsource comprehension. In the end, we

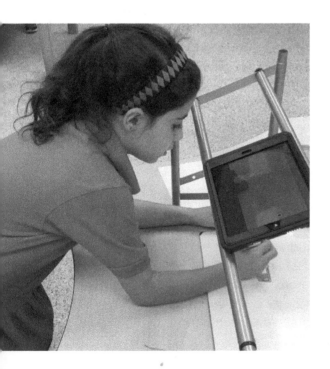

must teach our students transliteracy and shift their focus from simply reading and writing to developing and using *all* of the communication skills they'll need to achieve success in our modern society.

Think of what it takes to become a chef: If all chefs-in-training did was read cookbooks, take tests about what they read, and write about ingredients, chances are they probably wouldn't cook very well. The art of cooking requires understanding flavors, knowing which tools to use for which purposes, and being familiar with the different ways to develop a dish.

Until would-be chefs actually experiment with recipes, it is difficult for them to truly know how to cook. They must prove their ability to cook before they are called chefs. So how could they possibly learn how to become chefs if they have a teacher who believes experimenting with spices and herbs is a distraction?

The same principle applies to learning. Instead of simply reading the cookbook, start cooking—or, in our case, join Twitter. And if Twitter isn't for you, follow some blogs or create an Instagram account so you can better understand where your students are and how you can turn these social media platforms into a powerful learning tools within your classroom.

Being a disruptive teacher means understanding that although students know how to use technology, they don't understand how to use it to *learn*. It means speaking social media and understanding connected learning—and realizing the profound impact of both.

As teachers, we need to curate a network of educators who are doing great things in their classrooms, a network of colleagues who will introduce us to ideas and innovations, and people whom we can reach out to with questions. We should follow experts and learners alike who share creative ideas for helping our students become life-ready.

Connecting will serve as your roadmap, and your colleagues will become your guides—your own personal Sherpas—to creating a more innovative, disruptive classroom, where learning once again becomes a more relevant endeavor and literacy is transformed. Only once we *know* better can we *do* better.

> "I did then what I knew how to do. Now that I know better, I do better."
>
> **—Maya Angelou**

Ten Characteristics
OF OUR LEARNERS

1

They are the first real digital natives. They have never known a world without smartphones, tablets, and social media.

They expect technology; they need dynamic, interactive content; and they want to create more than just PowerPoint presentations.

2

They talk in images (e.g., emojis, pictures, and videos).

Find ways to use Canva, Flipgrid, and photo apps in your classroom and allow students to explain their understanding using pictures, graphs, and **infographics**.

3

They are social entrepreneurs and like their learning to have meaning and purpose.

You can nurture their passions by allowing them to do Genius Hour or **20% Time** projects or even create a real business.

** Bold/underlined words are defined in "Ideas to Try" on page 19.

We generally define "Generation Z" as people born between 1995 and 2010. However, some thought leaders claim Gen Z is less of a generation and more of a mindset that we can all adopt—if we aspire to learn, unlearn, and relearn.

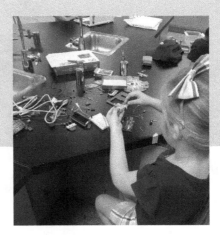

4 They think in 4-D, 360-degree, and high-definition videos.

Bringing **Google Expeditions** into your classroom is a great idea! Better yet, buy a **Ricoh Theta** and have students create their own **360-degree video** content.

5 They prefer to do hands-on and interactive projects.

Consider having students do projects that are in line with their learning style, like something musical or kinesthetic, or have them learn to code using apps like Scratch or Google's CS First (cs-first.com).

Ten Characteristics
OF OUR LEARNERS

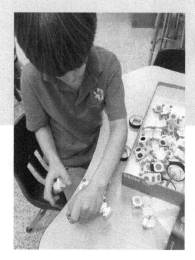

6
They communicate in short, bite-sized ideas.

Allow students to tweet with authors. Teach them how to write effective comments and reviews. Try the **100-Word Challenge** and the **Six-Word Summary**.

7
They like to create.

You can empower students by introducing **design thinking** and **coding** in your lessons.

8
Their social circle is global.

Allow students to connect with experts and peers who are from other geographical areas and have different perspectives. This allows them to crowdsource their learning, and teaches them empathy and how to harness the power of collaboration.

9

Their cell phones are the hub of their social lives, with their apps of choice being Snapchat, Instagram, and Houseparty.

Consider ways to safely introduce these apps into your classroom. Try **BookSnaps** or **SnapStories**.

10

They want to win using strategies, practice, and do-overs.

You can help them win by teaching learning strategies such as **sketchnoting** and by **gamifying** your classroom.

Constructivism and Connectivism

Clearly, your Generation Z students are primed for learning that integrates technology. As you design your lessons, consider how drawing upon the constructivism and connectivism learning theories could help you effectively deliver instruction in a way that meets your twenty-first-century learners' needs and expectations while also helping prepare them for their future. Here's a quick recap of these two theories and how they might help you improve the learning experiences in your classrooms.

Constructivism is based on the idea that students construct knowledge and meaning through experiences. Students need to work with information, play with it, try new ways, figure things out on their own (and in their own way), find other views and opinions, and come to their own understanding of concepts. In addition, they need to construct their own understanding and knowledge by reflecting on those experiences. Constructivism is based in Jean Piaget's theory of cognitive development which states that humans cannot be fed or given information for learning. Instead, we must construct knowledge.

A Constructivist Classroom

- Places students at the center
- Is activity-based
- Is noisy and full of movement
- Encourages students to become expert learners
- Includes problem-based learning
- Applies real-world problems to concepts
- Allows time for reflection
- Values meaning over facts

- Offers differentiated activities that build upon students' strengths and weaknesses
- Wants students to construct knowledge and create demonstrations of learning, not memorize and recite facts
- Has students taking on a major role in determining the direction of their learning and what that learning process looks like

Connectivism proposes that students learn through their connections and networks, both physical and digital. Developed by Canadian researchers Stephen Downes, the originator of the MOOC (Massive Open Online Course) and George Seimens, author of the book *Knowing Knowledge*, connectivism theory suggests that learning happens when students consult a diversity of opinions, use networks to find and validate relevant, up-to-date information, and utilize a crowd as the source of information. As educators, we must teach our students how to learn in a world where their social network can become a direct or even unintended teacher. Likewise, we must teach them how to critically think their way through the process and understand these new modes of learning.

A Connectivist Classroom

- Encourages students to blog with people from around the world

- Acknowledges the power of Twitter to grow a community of people passionate about a subject

- Allows students to publish their work in portfolios and gather feedback

- Encourages students to write collaboratively with peers from other countries

- Makes **Mystery Hangouts** (or Mystery Skypes), during which students guess their Skype partner's location, commonplace

- Teaches students how to effectively find and validate information online

- Elicits a variety of opinions through Twitter, Instagram, and blogs

- Understands how to find new, important learning channels

Making Thinking Visible
GIVING EVERY STUDENT A VOICE
AND SHARING STUDENTS' WORK

Throughout this book, you'll find three core ideas that we believe are essential to education: making thinking visible, giving every student a voice, and allowing students to share their work. Having worked in technology-infused classrooms for the past two decades, we've concluded that effective technology integration happens when educators ask themselves these questions:

- How can I make student thinking visible?

- How can I use the technology to hear from every student in the class?

- How can I allow students to actively share their work so that they can learn from one another?

When students are allowed to use technology to write papers or take notes, it certainly making their lives easier, but replacing pen and paper with technology doesn't equate to making real advances in the way we use technology in schools. Our goal (we hope yours, as well) is to ensure that we're using technology in ways that will help students **make bigger gains in their academic growth** and also **allow us to understand where they are in their learning process** so we can quickly make changes in our instructional coaching and help them succeed. That means their thinking and learning must be visible.

Making Thinking (and Learning) Visible

In the past, it was difficult to help our students visualize their thinking because we didn't have time to hear from each and every student and listen to their reflections very often. But thanks to today's technology, getting inside our students' heads—and finding out what they know and don't know—is easier than ever. We can ask students to reveal their insights by offering the use of apps that allow them to articulate and record their learning experiences, ideas, and thinking. This is especially important because at the foundation of all good, cognitive

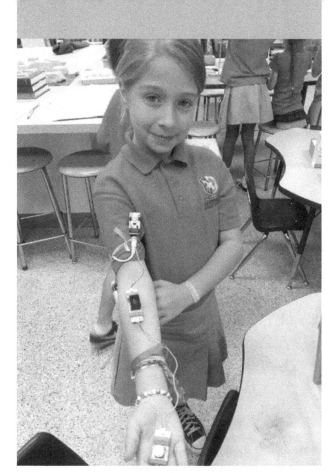

learning is the idea that we must teach our students how to think about thinking (**metacognition**). Fortunately, our Gen Z students are characterized by their ability to learn, unlearn, and relearn ideas and concepts. Because our information landscape is rapidly changing, this ability is growing in importance and becoming even more essential to teach.

To understand how students learn best, though, we must first learn how to make their thinking visible by using "thinking routines," or methods for questioning the learning process. In their book, *Making Thinking Visible*, authors Ron Ritchhart, Mark Church, and Karin Morrison describe these thinking routines, many of which classrooms use to uncover the root of the thinking process. Take, for example, this key thinking routine from their book, which shows us how students' thinking has changed: "I used to think ... but now I think..." The key here is making these processes part of the very fabric of our classrooms so that students intuitively activate them to make connections and deepen their reflections. This book will show you how to easily integrate technology tools in ways that will allow for deeper reflective learning and help students better understand their own thinking and learning processes.

Thinking routines remind us that learning is not a product, but a *process* of understanding. During that process, we should encourage our students to verbalize and explain what they're learning, as well as what is and isn't working, what struggles they're facing, what comes easily, and whether they believe they've reached the learning target. At that point, they should offer demonstrations of their learning to show they've reached the goal. We also call these demonstrations of learning "assessments for learning," and students should do them throughout their learning process so they can gain insights into how they learn best.

In all likelihood, your classroom is filled with technology. The ideas and tools discussed in this book will help you use that technology to quickly and efficiently unveil your students' thinking and understanding.

Student Voice

Think back to when you were a student. There were probably about four or five of your peers who always raised their hands first to answer any question. As a result, your teacher heard from these eager students frequently but had limited information about where the rest of the students in the class were in the learning process.

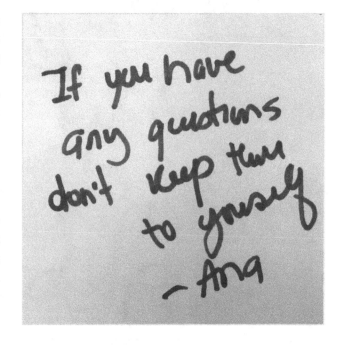

Beyond having the obvious problem of getting everyone's active participation, the tools traditionally used to gather information about students' learning, like fill-in-the-blank and multiple-choice questions, don't give us a good opportunity to really understand our students as individuals, but, rather, as kids who complete tasks. Based on these answers, we learn very little about how students come to their conclusions or about what they really understand.

Thanks to technology, though, we can now ask a question of and hear from *every* child in the room, even the ones who are too shy or too scared to answer out loud. We can do this in about two minutes, which is less time than it would take to gather answers from those with their hands up and even less time than it takes to write down an answer.

 Check out this site for a quick-start guide and resource on thinking routines:

Bit.ly/GICThinking.

For example, when we were kids, our teachers would have us respond to questions by writing the answers on a piece of paper, then tell us to place the paper with the answers upside-down, pass them forward, and sit quietly as they were collected. It was as if we were sharing top-secret information only our teacher could read. Days would pass before we received feedback, and by the time the teacher knew if we understood the lesson, class was long over. Sadly, even the interval she spent collecting the papers resulted in lost learning time. Thankfully, today's technology and tools have changed all that.

If you aren't hearing from every student in your class during crucial learning segments, it may be because you're not using technology to its full abilities. The great news is you can! For example, using an app like Socrative, you can ask a "Quick Question" from the Launchpad. Students enter your virtual room and quickly respond to the prompt. As the responses populate on the screen, you can easily ascertain what the students have learned and where some understanding may still be lacking. With this information, you can adjust your lesson in real time—based on the individual needs of your students.

Sharing Student Work

When we use technology to upgrade our learning, it can have profound effects on students. Take sharing student work, for example: By incorporating visual thinking apps like Padlet, Socrative, and See-Saw into this process, students can watch their peers' responses come in, compare their answers, make adjustments to incorrect thinking, and maybe even learn something from the posted answers. It's during this sharing process that students are plunged into a state of **metacognition**—when they are thinking about their thinking.

We realize traditional teaching methods often frown upon students seeing one another's answers, but this is a learning fallacy, and it's one that needs to change. Keeping student work private ignores the foundational theory of Constructivism, which states that people construct knowledge and meaning from their experiences. (See page 12.) In short, students learn best from one another, and seeing another student's answers can often result in important "light bulb" moments.

Additionally, students want to put their best foot forward when they know their work will be seen by someone other than their teacher. You'll notice that when your students know their work will be shared with the class, the school, or even with the world online, they will begin taking the time to construct very critical, well-thought-out responses.

Employing these three techniques—making thinking visible, using technology to hear from every student, and allowing students to share their work—affects student growth in a way that empowers them to understand *how* they learn. In effect, they learn about learning. When we combine these techniques with having students create demonstrations of learning to reflect on their learning process, such as explaining how they met the target, that's when the magic really happens. It's then that technology becomes something more than a word processor or powerful Internet searcher—it amplifies the learning process.

Ideas to Try
IN *YOUR* CLASSROOM
AND GLOSSARY OF TERMS

As you progress through the book, you may find you are not familiar with a few terms. In an effort to make the information more clear, we have provided this glossary of ideas to try that will serve as a reference and a place to find more information on the ideas presented.

100 Word Challenge

This is a weekly creative writing challenge based on a prompt, which can be a picture or a series of words. In just one hundred words, students must write a creative response then share it on the 100 Word Challenge website (100WC.net). They can then share, view, and comment on examples from around the globe. Visit 100WC.net for more information.

20% Time

The "20% Time" concept was originally based on Google's allowing its employees to spend 20 percent of their time working on special projects related to their personal interests. Today, many schools have adopted it by giving students 20 percent of class time to explore self-directed studies similar to passion projects.

360-Degree Videos

This is a video that offers the watcher a 360-degree view—a video that can be touched and moved with a touchscreen or can be manipulated with a mouse to drag the video around on a non-touchscreen device. Instead of looking straight at the focus of the picture, you have the ability to move the video and see what is happening all around the object—to get a full view. Check out a great example of a 360-degree video of a mega-coaster at bit.ly/GICExamples, making sure to drag the screen to see the entire view.

BookSnaps

BookSnaps are the perfect way to engage your students in the reading process. Using the very popular social networking app Snapchat, students read, pick a passage to engage with (connect with the content), snap a picture of the passage, doodle on it to show meaning (show their thinking), then share it with their peers. Students could also take a photo of their favorite quote and highlight it using words or a bitmoji or even create a meme. You can use Seesaw as an alternative for younger students. Check out #BookSnaps as well as founder Tara Martin's Twitter page (@TaraMartinEDU) for creative ideas.

Click and Listens

To convey student thinking in a fun, creative way, have students choose a bitmoji that represents an idea, emotion, or anything else they want to communicate. They can then use the Google Chrome Extension Talk and Comment to record themselves giving an explanation. They then take the link provided by Talk and Comment and add it as a hyperlink to the bitmoji (or any image).

Coding

Coding is a set of instructions or rules we write using one of the many programming languages to create computer software, apps, and websites that computers can understand. Coding promotes critical thinking and understanding of if/then scenarios.

Design Thinking

Design thinking is a human- or student-centered process based on empathy that is used to help solve problems and find solutions. Many students and schools use the design thinking model set forth by Stanford's d.school.

Differentiate

Differentiating instruction is based on the idea that you need to determine where your students are in their learning process through formative assessments, then design your lessons and resources to meet their learning styles and growth trajectory. The Differentiated School author, Carol Tomlinson, Ed.D., calls this "active planning for and attention to student differences in classrooms."

Freemium

This describes a software or web service that provides some of its services for free but charges to access its premium features.

Gamify

Gamification means applying gaming strategies and game-design techniques to the classroom to engage and motivate your students.

Google Expeditions

Thanks to Google Cardboard and the Expeditions app, students can take field trips without ever leaving the classroom. The Expeditions app has a series of collections that take students to places like museums, major attractions, underwater, and outer space, all through virtual reality. Google Expeditions currently offers students more than a hundred locations to visit.

HyperDocs

HyperDocs are based in Google Docs with curated links that move students through a lesson design. It allows you to package lesson plans with your students in mind; create learning experiences that emphasize how students learn, rather than simply what they learn; and take advantage of the many web resources available. (For more information about HyperDocs, check out page 13 of The HyperDoc Handbook, written by Lisa Highfill, Kelly Hilton, and Sarah Landis.)

Infographics

Infographics are images representing data or information in an easy-to-read, visually appealing way.

InsertLearning

This Google Chrome browser Extension allows you to turn any website into an interactive lesson and add YouTube videos, questions, or media. InsertLearning is a great way to provide students with opportunities for discussion and differentiation.

Learning Journals

A learning journal lets students keep track of their learning over time, allowing them and you to get a longitudinal view of their progress.

Metacognition

Literally translated from Greek, metacognition means beyond meaning. It is the process of going beyond learning and moving toward gaining an awareness and understanding of our thought processes or, more simply put, thinking about thinking.

Multiple Intelligences

Harvard University professor Howard Gardner, Ph.D., proposes that instead of a single IQ, humans possess many types of intelligence, each representing a different way of processing information. These intelligences include verbal-linguistic, logical-mathematical, visual-spatial, musical, naturalistic, bodily-kinesthetic, interpersonal, and intrapersonal.

Mystery Hangouts

A Mystery Hangout (or Mystery Skype) brings two classes together, with each class developing a series of educated questions to help them intelligently deduce the location of the other class or school. In this scenario, kids get to apply and use geographical knowledge, critical thinking, and the skill of deduction to figure out where the other students are located. Most teachers structure this activity around the twenty questions model and have students ask each other one question at a time about their geographical location.

Philosophical Chairs

Similar to a debate, Philosophical Chairs is a kinesthetic activity built around constructing knowledge. Start by giving your students a central topic or question that they must choose to agree or disagree with, or remain neutral about. Students then either stand or sit in areas designated as "agree," "disagree," or "neutral." One at a time, students speak, trying to convince their peers that their side is the right one. As their peers hear the statements, they can change their position and move to the other areas. This exciting activity typically lasts about twenty minutes and ends with a reflection or debrief of some sort.

Reading Fluency Journals

Students capture their reading fluency by recording themselves reading a story that has been placed on the screen of an app—in this case, we recommend Explain Everything. Using the pointer tool, students progress though the story on the screen as the app records their voice reading the excerpt. They do this several times during the year to capture a longitudinal journal of their reading abilities and growth.

Ricoh Theta

The Ricoh Theta is a 360-degree camera that takes photos and records videos. Most of the camera's controls live on its smartphone app, meaning you can place the camera in different locations using a selfie stick or tripod then step away and snap a picture or video using your phone. Your phone then houses the content until you publish or share it to another location.

Screencasts

A screencast (or screen capture) is a digital recording of a screen and often lets you narrate what you're seeing and thinking.

Six-Word Summaries

This technique requires students to think critically about which six words best summarize an activity, idea, or information—think of it as profound brevity. Sample task: Summarize your favorite book in six words.

Sketchnoting

Sketchnoting is a strategy where students draw pictures and write words in a way that connects to the information or captures a theme, using an app like ProCreate.

SnapStories

Students write a story's narrative with Snaps (from Snapchat) they take during the course of a single day. These snaps serve as the inspiration and brainstorming for a story they will write.

Student Agency

This is a form of deeper learning that requires students to think, question, pursue, and create to take ownership of their learning.

Video Reflective Journals

These are chronological, diary-like collections of student learning. They house students' video reflections of their thinking, reading fluency, and even language or content acquisition. Over time, students refer back to these journals. We recommend making these reflective recordings using screencasting or Explain Everything and then placing them in Book Creator.

Word Studies

Word Studies serve as an alternative to the traditional spelling instruction, in that they're based on students learning word patterns, rather than memorizing unconnected words. Go to ReadingRockets.org for more information.

Before you integrate technology into your classroom, ask yourself these questions:

1. Is my goal to teach the technology or the content?

2. Is this form of technology how my student learns best? Does it support their learning abilities?

3. Are all of my students doing the same project? If they are, is that the best way for each individual learner to demonstrate their understanding of the learning targets?

4. Am I using the technology to amplify skills like collaboration, consumption, or critical thinking? Does the tool encourage students to be curious or create?

5. How does using the technology give me rich information about the student's learning and growth? What new and insightful information can I gather about the learner from the project?

6. Am I integrating technology for the sake of integrating technology, or to make my lessons better, more powerful, more collaborative, and easier to access from outside the classroom?

7. Will the technology empower my students to do things I'd never imagined, things that go beyond my classroom's four walls when I was a student?

8. Have my students received any instruction on how to use the tool? Do they know what good design looks like? Have I talked to them about fonts? Do they know how to make insightful and meaningful comments?

9. Do my students know how to effectively search for and validate information online?

10. How are the social media and blog posts I'm asking my students to write driving learning and curiosity in my class?

A Quick Look
AT UbD

Understanding by Design (UbD) is based on the belief that teachers should design instruction backwards. It is a three-step process that **identifies the desired results, determines the acceptable evidence**, and **plans the learning experiences and instruction accordingly**. The framework gives teachers the flexibility to allow each student to progress toward this learning target in different ways. You might start with an essential question that students work toward answering, whether that's a student-generated question or one you've crafted for the unit.

According to ASCD UbD White Paper from March 2012, "Backward design encourages teachers and curriculum planners to first think like assessors before designing specific units and lessons. The assessment evidence we need reflects the desired results identified."[1]

Students need to be able to show their understanding and progression toward the learning goal, and according to the UbD framework, they do this through the lens of the six facets of understanding:

1. They can **explain** the learning goal.

2. They **interpret** it.

3. They **apply** it.

4. They can **understand different perspectives**.

5. They **show empathy**.

6. They **demonstrate a metacognitive awareness** of the material and their learning.

McTighe and Wiggins explain that the main goal of the student is "transfer of learning" and making meaning of the experience.

This framework will be the basis of the next four sections, how we approach the desired results we are looking for, and the way we view learning.

---

1 McTighe, Jay and Grant Wiggins, " Understanding by Design Framework." ASCD.org, http://www.ascd.org/ASCD/pdf/siteASCD/publications/UbD_WhitePaper0312.pdf.

Assessment
FOR/AS/OF LEARNING

Before we begin our roadmap to effective technology integration, here is a breakdown of Assessment For/As/Of Learning

Assessment for Learning

An **assessment *for* learning,** or formative assessment, is exactly what it sounds like: It's an assessment that helps us understand where our students are in the learning process. However, in this case, we don't grade these assessments. Rather, when done properly, they provide us and each of our students with ongoing, real-time feedback about where they are in their learning and what interventions they may need to achieve success. These assessments also allow us to make just-in-time adjustments to our classroom instruction and provide students with valuable insights into which areas they may need to focus their attention.

Assessment as Learning

An **assessment *as* learning** is an ongoing assessment that students do to reflect on and monitor their progress. By asking students to record their reflections and processes using a tool like Screencastify, we're encouraging them to think about their learning process, make their thinking visible, and help them take responsibility for achieving their personal learning goals. By doing this type of assessment, students are more likely to ask for and receive feedback from others. This feedback can be critical to helping them understand their own areas of strength and need.

Assessment of Learning

An **assessment *of* learning** is the "summative evaluation" of a student's work. In this case, we measure a student's work against the predetermined learning criteria to see if they've demonstrated an understanding of the intended learning targets. Generally, students' final creations and work give us more insight into their learning and personal growth than an assessment based in multiple-choice questions ever could.

Consideration: Typically, summative assessments that take place at the end of a unit and look at a standardized proficiency, judging individual students by everyone else's progress. Instead of asking the same questions and having a blanket target for all of our students, though, we should look for student growth on an individual scale. We should find out what each student knows at the beginning of a unit then determine individualized targets. This allows us to throw out percentages and measure our well-defined learning targets against the student-led conferences and evidence of learning we glean from their portfolios, thereby letting us grade each student on their individual growth, not where we expect everyone to be.

Pedagogy +
TOOLS TO USE

Well-planned instructional design is the foundation of good teaching. As we've discussed, the better insight you have into your students' understanding, the better able you will be to design a learning experience that meets their needs. In the next sections, we are going to look at how we can use technology to make student thinking visible by using technology tools. The journey begins with formative assessment using tools that target student thinking and allow you to hear from every student in the class. Next, based on data you collect from the formative assessment pieces, you will most likely discover that students are progressing in different ways and that you need to offer them different and targeted resources to help them make the most of their learning strengths. This step includes giving students an individualized means of showing growth with demonstrations of learning. Finally, we will explore the importance of reflection.

All of these processes will be based in the Understanding by Design framework for teaching by Jay McTighe and Grant Wiggins. This framework is meant to help teachers (1) identify the learning goals, (2) determine what evidence will prove students have met their goals, and (3) begin planning instruction. This is called "beginning with the end in mind," and is a researched-based approach on how students can show us their learning and understanding.

Formative Assessment

Tips for Differentiation

Demonstrations of Learning

Reflection and Curation

Formative Assessment
AND THE TOOLS TO USE

WHY WE DO THIS: As discussed earlier, an assessment *for* learning, or formative assessment, is exactly what it sounds like: It's an assessment that helps teachers understand where their students are in the learning process. Following the principles of *Understanding by Design*, formative assessment is where we look for acceptable evidence toward the learning goal. These assessments are not meant for grading. They are meant to give us some indicator of where the students are in the learning process. We don't grade formative assessments, because students deserve the opportunity to fully develop, make mistakes, and learn before they are graded on the material.

When done properly, these assessments provide us and our students with ongoing, real-time feedback about where they are in their learning and what interventions they may need in order to achieve success. These assessments also allow us to make just-in-time adjustments to our classroom instruction and provide students with valuable insights into which areas they may need to focus their attention. The sooner the student understands how they did on these assessments, the better. That is why we seek to make student thinking visible in this process—not only to the teacher but also to the students themselves. Formative assessments provide opportunities for students to engage in metacognitive reflection on their learning; it's during these activities that they can start thinking about their thinking and making their own adjustments as well. If done correctly, each formative assessment should lead the students down a path where their understanding and performance grow closer and closer to the learning target.

> "The more you teach without finding out who understands the concepts and who doesn't, the greater the likelihood that only already-proficient students will succeed."
>
> —Grant Wiggins

Strategy

Here is where we make student thinking visible. Formative assessment is crucial to understanding what they know, what they have learned, or where they might still need further help.

FIRST, it's time to check in and see where your students are in their learning process. These are informal checks and not meant to be graded.

NEXT, depending upon the learning target, you might choose one of the tools in this section to help make your student's thinking visible. Each tool will provide a different avenue for achieving this. For example, Socrative is best for text-based answers, Padlet for having students provide graphical representations of learning, and Talk and Comment are for audio-based information. Each of the tools provides a wide range of different opportunities to gather rich information about student learning and growth.

FINALLY, based on the types of data these tools provide, you might find that you need to change your instruction or begin the process of differentiation.

Tools:

Socrative

Padlet

Google Forms

Formative

Talk and Comment

SOCRATIVE

GOOGLE INFUSION: Socrative with Google Drive

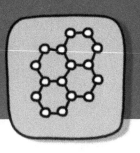

WHAT IS SOCRATIVE? Socrative is a website and app that allows you to quickly gather information about your students' learning in the form of closed and open-ended questions. There is also a game-like response area called "Space Race." For our purposes, we will discuss the Quick Question option. This option is one of the choices found on the app's Launchpad, or front page.

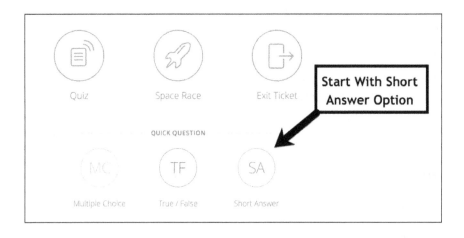

GREAT BECAUSE ... it allows you to hear from every student in your class, not just the few who raise their hands to answer questions.

SET UP IS ... EASY. The website's interface is simple, and you can navigate it without prior setup. (Go to bit.ly/GoogleInfusedClassroom for a tutorial.)

ALLOWS YOU TO ... make all of your students' thinking visible by asking an open-ended question. You can gather student responses in one stream, then keep and dissect responses later for further data.

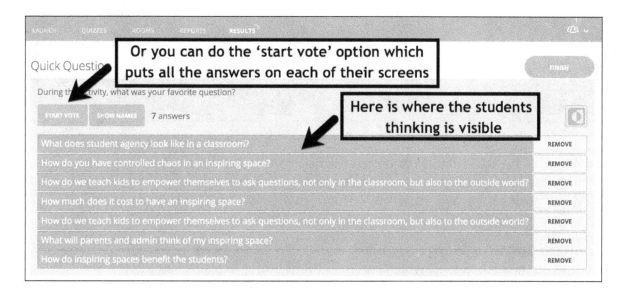

Or you can do the 'start vote' option which puts all the answers on each of their screens

Here is where the students thinking is visible

GIVES YOU THIS INFORMATION … students' answers appear on the screen, allowing them to compare their responses with their peers' as they finish. Plus, Socrative gives you access to a saved copy of your class's responses for later.

WHAT'S GREAT IS THAT … students enter a state of metacognition as they think about one another's answers in comparison to their own, prompting them to continue learning even after they've responded. This tool also allows students to vote on the best answer from everyone's responses.

SHOWS YOU THE INFORMATION … in a simple stream. Socrative's interactive approach is fun and chock-full of important data.

MATH–Have students tell you in their own words how they would solve a math problem. This addresses Common Core standards that asks students to explain how they would solve a math problem.

LANGUAGE ARTS–Doing a response to Literature? Have students share out their thesis statements. This way they can see each other's ideas and you can gauge where they are in the process.

PADLET

GOOGLE INFUSION: Padlet with Google Classroom

WHAT IS PADLET? Padlet is both a website and a Chrome Extension that lets you create a blank digital wall where you can gather student work, answers, or any other type of information that will help inform your teaching.

GREAT BECAUSE … unlike Socrative, Padlet lets students easily add images to their responses, which can help them better explain their ideas visually.

SET UP IS … EASY. The tool's interface requires little setup and only asks that you choose the type of wall (freeform, grid, stream, canvas, or shelf) and the background you'd like to use. Students then join the wall through a bit.ly URL, Google Classroom share, or **HyperDoc**.

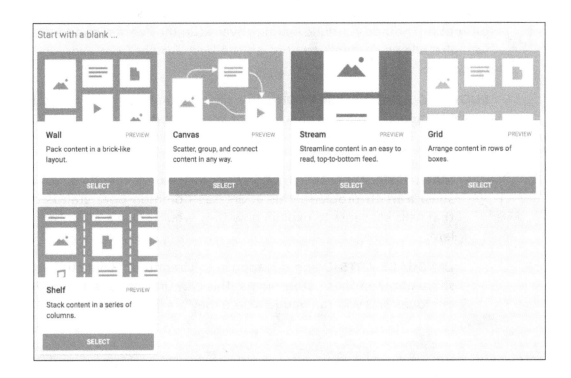

Start with a blank …

Wall — PREVIEW
Pack content in a brick-like layout.
SELECT

Canvas — PREVIEW
Scatter, group, and connect content in any way.
SELECT

Stream — PREVIEW
Streamline content in an easy to read, top-to-bottom feed.
SELECT

Grid — PREVIEW
Arrange content in rows of boxes.
SELECT

Shelf — PREVIEW
Stack content in a series of columns.
SELECT

ALLOWS YOU TO ... make student thinking visible and share their creations through images, graphs, and text, which are placed on the Padlet and then projected onto a screen for their peers to see.

GIVES YOU THIS INFORMATION ... on the Padlet wall and students' can save and refer to their responses both during and after their learning process.

WHAT'S GREAT IS THAT ... it makes the teaching world your oyster. It lets you add content-specific backgrounds, gives students the ability to add videos and graphics, and provides a much more visual representation of learning.

SHOWS YOU THE INFORMATION IN THIS WAY ... Padlet displays one simple wall, where a student's work can be easily seen and shared.

 USE PADLET AS AN EXIT TICKET—Ask students to share three things they learned in class that day.

Ask students to create a Six-Word Summary on Canva—Have them upload the Canva graphic to Padlet to share with you or the class.

Islamic Art
Colorful
Geometric Pattern
Spain to Saudi Arabia

GOOGLE FORMS

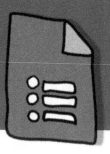

GOOGLE INFUSION: Google Forms and Wordle

WHAT ARE GOOGLE FORMS? Google Forms are part of the G Suite of apps. You can collect student responses, then display them as graphs or on a spreadsheet, creating a quick and easy way to view data.

GREAT BECAUSE ... it allows students to quickly answer questions. Then you can display their responses on a screen or whiteboard. These responses can begin a discussion or help you determine how to modify your teaching.

SET UP IS ... INTERMEDIATE. Of the five tools, this is one of the more difficult to set up, as you need to populate the form with questions before you begin your lesson. (In comparison, you can use Socrative and Padlet on the fly.) Once you've created your form, you can share it with students through Google Classroom.

ALLOWS YOU TO ... take the students' responses you've collected through Google Forms and use them to **differentiate** your upcoming instruction or throw them into a word cloud, such as a Wordle, which can kick off a class discussion or a fun activity called **Philosophical Chairs**.

GIVES YOU THIS INFORMATION … Forms create a spreadsheet and a graphical representation of responses. Both can be found in the "Responses" section of the form, and require nothing more than creating the spreadsheet or scrolling down to view graphical results.

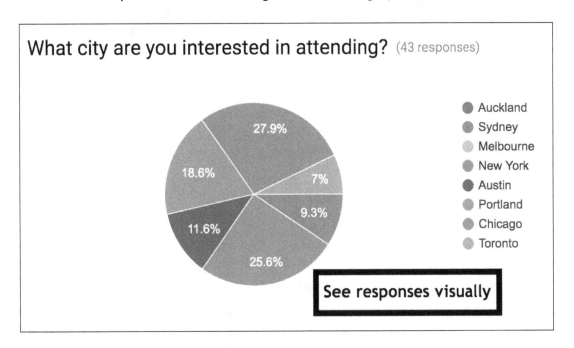

What city are you interested in attending? (43 responses)

- 27.9%
- 18.6%
- 7%
- 9.3%
- 11.6%
- 25.6%

Legend:
- Auckland
- Sydney
- Melbourne
- New York
- Austin
- Portland
- Chicago
- Toronto

See responses visually

WHAT'S GREAT IS THAT … you can do a lot with the information in a spreadsheet and even share the results with your students so they can keep track of their own growth.

SHOWS YOU THE INFORMATION IN THIS WAY … Google Forms displays the data it collects as spreadsheet cells or graphs.

USE A GOOGLE FORM TO HAVE STUDENTS PROVIDE FIVE WORDS TO DESCRIBE A STORY—Throw the responses into a word cloud and put it on the screen to start a start a discussion about which words are repeated and why.

CREATE AN EXIT TICKET—When you need the exit ticket to be more private, use Google Forms.

FORMATIVE

GOOGLE INFUSION: Formative and Google Classroom
(or even Google Slides)

WHAT IS FORMATIVE? Formative is a powerful web-based tool that's perfect for gathering information about student learning. It offers students multiple ways to respond, including the ability to write on their screens. This then allows them to see the process they went through to solve a problem, such as a math equation.

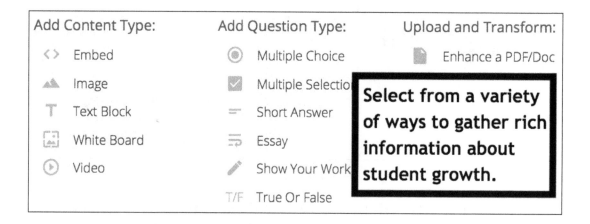

Add Content Type:	Add Question Type:	Upload and Transform:
‹› Embed	⊙ Multiple Choice	📄 Enhance a PDF/Doc
⛰ Image	☑ Multiple Selectio	
T Text Block	═ Short Answer	**Select from a variety of ways to gather rich information about student growth.**
🖼 White Board	⇶ Essay	
▶ Video	✏ Show Your Work	
	T/F True Or False	

GREAT BECAUSE … it offers a variety of ways to collect information about student learning using any device.

SET UP IS … INTERMEDIATE. In most cases, you'll need to plan and prepare the questions within Formative before class begins. Students can log in to Formative with their G Suite account or using an assignment code—which makes it fairly easy for you to use with your classes.

ALLOWS YOU TO … quickly gather both text-based and graphical information about your students' learning and growth. With that information, you can better provide students with resources to assist in understanding concepts with which they may be struggling.

GIVES YOU THIS INFORMATION … in a dashboard environment so you can see numerous responses in one place.

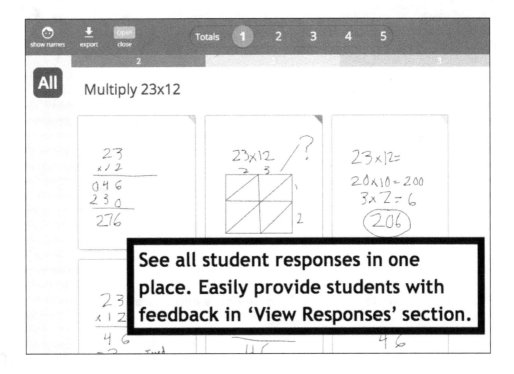

See all student responses in one place. Easily provide students with feedback in 'View Responses' section.

WHAT'S GREAT IS THAT … it lets you provide feedback to students from the dashboard, both individually and as an entire class.

USE THE 'SHOW YOUR WORK' OPTION to have students show how they solved a math problem.

TEACHING ABOUT THE CIVIL WAR? Give students a copy of the map of the United States and have students identify the Mason Dixon line by drawing its precise location.

TALK AND COMMENT

GOOGLE INFUSION: Talk and Comment Extension
with Google Docs or Slides

WHAT IS TALK AND COMMENT? Talk and Comment is a Chrome extension that (once installed) lives all the way to the right, middle side of every website, including Google Docs and Slides.

Finish recording and press the check

Students use the tool to record voice notes and share those notes using the link provided.

click to record

WHAT'S GREAT IS THAT ... this is an easily accessible tool that can help you quickly find out what a student has learned, is thinking, or may want to know more about.

SET UP IS ... EASY. Students simply look for a round clear button on the side of the page, click it, (it automatically starts recording on click) then start explaining their learning in their own words. They might do this in a Google Doc to explain their writing, or a in a Google Slide to explain their choice of graphics—giving the teacher insights they may not have had without the tool.

ALLOWS YOU TO ... quickly access your students' explanations so you can understand what they've learned.

GIVES YOU THIS INFORMATION ... students' recordings are turned into links that can be placed as a comment in Google Docs or Slides or turned in to you for review using a form or Google Classroom. What is fun is that once a student places their link in a comment, the link automagically becomes a play button.

WHAT'S GREAT IS THAT … Talk and Comment allows students to express themselves orally, which may be easier for those students who find writing their thoughts difficult.

SHOWS YOU THE INFORMATION IN THIS WAY … via a link to the recording and allows you to listen to your students' explanations of what they've learned or have questions about.

TAKE AUDIO NOTES IN A GOOGLE DOC—Have students paste their Talk and Comment link into a comment in Google Docs. Press return and that link turns into a play button. This way they can take audio notes as they read.

HAVE THEM EXPLAIN THEIR UNDERSTANDING OF CONTENT—After reading an article online, have students select Talk and Comment and quickly tell you what the article was about. Turn in the link to that audio recording using a Google Form.

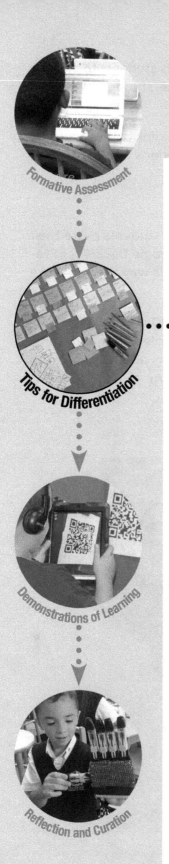

Formative Assessment

Tips for Differentiation

Demonstrations of Learning

Reflection and Curation

Tips for Differentiation
AND THE TOOLS TO USE

Now that you have done some formative assessment, you have hopefully gathered some important data about each of your students. Using the UbD framework, you'll be able to use that data to design instruction that helps each individual student meet the learning goal. It's time to take that data, analyze it, and uncover where students might be struggling, where they can jump ahead, and where they might need some additional resources. And what you're likely to discover is that your students are heading down the path of growth in very different ways.

Differentiation is crucial in learning. It recognizes the reality that everyone learns differently and that each child possesses unique learning abilities. The goal for us as educators is to teach to those strengths, not to the class as a whole. Simply put, differentiation is defined as the delivery model of instruction that best meets the needs of every student in the classroom.

Differentiation is a multi-dimensional and sometimes difficult concept to employ in traditional classroom settings. However, the tools and technology we'll discuss in this section will provide you a few examples of how you can use differentiation to amplify the learning process.

> "I never teach my pupils. I only attempt to provide the conditions in which they can learn."
>
> **–Albert Einstein**

Differentiation, as described by Carol Ann Tomlinson and Susan Demirsky Allan in their book *Leadership for Differentiating Schools and Classrooms*, is guided by three principals:

1. By respectful tasks that are inclusive of each child's learning style.

2. By flexible grouping where a student is grouped with peers who bring out the best in that child's learning experience and where a collaborative environment can flourish.

3. By continued assessment and adjustment of instruction by the teacher.

This section explores technology that allows you to deliver *respectful tasks* that are *inclusive* of each child's learning strength. By using the tools in this section, you can provide each and every one of your students with the resources that will better equip them to make meaning of the content.

For example, ask yourself...

- How do my students learn best?

- Would they most benefit from watching a video about the concept on their own so they can pause it and write down notes?

- Would reading about the lesson be helpful?

- Would a visual prompt like a concept map or picture help some of my students make sense of what they are learning?

The tools in this section will provide a way for you to easily deliver these differentiated resources to your students.

Strategy

First, use the information you have gathered from formative assessments to decide where the students are in the learning process.

Next, curate or create resources that would help that individual learner's needs. When done well, these resources will allow students to construct knowledge and empower their learning.

Finally, decide which platform you'll use to pass out the resources. (We've provided a few great examples on the next pages). These tools will help you differentiate the resources in a place your students can effortlessly access as needed.

Tools:

Classroom

HyperDocs

Google Sites

YouTube

GOOGLE CLASSROOM

GOOGLE INFUSION: Google Classroom to share almost any web-based tool

WHAT IS GOOGLE CLASSROOM? Google Classroom is an online platform for distributing and collecting student work through the Google ecosystem.

GREAT BECAUSE … it simplifies student workflow and the distribution of resources.

SET UP IS … INTERMEDIATE. Create a class, then invite your students (using a PIN or by email) to join.

THE TOOL OFFERS THIS INFORMATION … You can see who has turned in work, when they responded, and what work is still missing.

ALLOWS YOU TO … easily share resources with students in real time, then organize those resources by tagging posts, using keywords, that can be used for future retrieval

WHAT'S GREAT IS THAT … it allows you to differentiate student learning by providing a space where you can quickly and efficiently distribute resources, video tutorials, and related materials.

SHOWS YOU THE INFORMATION IN THIS WAY … Classroom works like a social media stream, in that students can always see the most recently shared resources at the top of the page.

INDIVIDUALIZE STUDENT ASSIGNMENTS—Pass out leveled assignments to different students. This can be done by selecting *all students* or checking the students you want to share the assignments with.

HYPERDOCS

GOOGLE INFUSION: Google Docs or Slides and almost any web-based tool

WHAT IS A HYPERDOC? A HyperDoc is a student-facing digital lesson plan you create and package using Google apps. When you curate resources for HyperDocs, the emphasis is on pedagogy and meeting individual students' needs.

GREAT BECAUSE ... you to create an entire digital resource document in one place. Students develop agency through exercising their voice and making choices as they make their way through the lesson.

SETUP IS ... INTERMEDIATE. In this case, though, the tool's difficulty level is dependent upon your preferences and how you decide to design and package lessons using resource links.

ALLOWS YOU TO ... curate multimedia resources, organize the flow of a lesson in one place, and guide students through the process of making their learning visible.

GIVES YOU THE INFORMATION ... in a well-crafted lesson. HyperDocs include blended learning strategies, self-paced learning, and differentiation.

WHAT'S GREAT IS THAT ... HyperDocs are ideal for all students, no matter their learning style or need.

SHOW YOU THE INFORMATION IN THIS WAY ... HyperDocs present information in an organized, appealing, and accessible way.

GOOGLE SITES

GOOGLE INFUSION: Google Sites and Google Drive

WHAT IS GOOGLE SITES? Google Sites is a collaborative web page creation platform in the G Suite of products.

GREAT BECAUSE ... you can create a web page to share all of your learning materials in a single, easy-to-access location. Google Sites would be a great tool to use if you wanted to collaborate with other teachers or classrooms.

SETUP IS ... INTERMEDIATE. Simply drag and drop elements into place on your web page and effortlessly upload items from the G Suite before publishing your work.

ALLOWS YOU TO ... collaborate, create, edit, and share. What's more, it works well with all of G Suite's apps, allowing you to easily publish the work on your Google Drive.

GIVES YOU THIS INFORMATION ... it creates a single, easy-to-access place that resembles a typical web page where students can access information inside and outside of class.

WHAT'S GREAT IS THAT ... you can edit Sites in real time, meaning you can quickly add to and change your resources to ensure you're helping students wherever they are in their learning process.

SHOWS YOU INFORMATION IN THIS WAY ... Google Sites displays information as a web page, complete with embedded links and products that students can access and use.

YOUTUBE

GOOGLE INFUSION: YouTube and Google Slides or Sites

WHAT IS YOUTUBE? YouTube is a video-hosting website that allows users to upload, view, share, edit, and comment on videos. It is also a powerful search engine and lets students subscribe to your curated channels.

GREAT BECAUSE ... you can create content, then share it on your own channel and/or as part of a curated playlist.

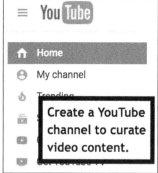

Create a YouTube channel to curate video content.

SET UP IS ... EASY. Just go to the arrow icon in the upper-right-hand corner of the screen, click it, then select the videos you'd like to upload. Once you've uploaded a file, you can also edit it, if needed.

ALLOWS YOU TO ... create a playlist by using the "Add to" icon at the bottom of the your channel home page. You can even add videos other YouTube users have created to your playlist.

GIVES YOU THIS INFORMATION ... If your channel is set to private, you can find out how many views your video has from just your students and how long your visitors watched it. You can also embed links to further resources within your videos, or in the information section, and add closed captioning for those students who need the extra assistance.

WHAT'S GREAT IS THAT ... YouTube saves your large video files to a digital cloud so your students can access these resources outside the classroom and you don't have to take up storage space on your computer.

SHOWS YOU INFORMATION IN THIS WAY ... YouTube presents the videos you've created and curated in a playlist stream.

 Students struggling with Math? Create a playlist of " Khan Academy" tutorials or better yet...create a playlist of *student* created tutorials.

Students struggling with directions? Create a video explaining the instructions for those students who need the auditory and visual help.

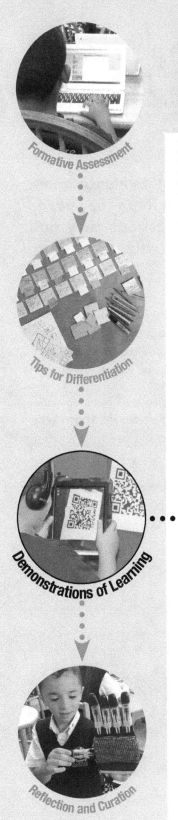

Formative Assessment

Tips for Differentiation

Demonstrations of Learning

Reflection and Curation

Demonstrations
OF LEARNING

Up to this point, we've discussed the value of gathering information through formative assessments and using that data to differentiate learning. We've explored ways to provide each child with "respectful tasks" and resources that will help them move closer to their learning goals. It's now time to empower students to show both their "transfer of learning" and how they made meaning of the content. In other words, it's time for students to demonstrate their learning.

To ensure students create meaningful demonstrations of learning, the methods they use must be multifaceted and layered. Thankfully, technology allows students to demonstrate their learning in authentic and rich ways. It provides us with the opportunity to hear from every student, uncover their thinking, visualize the steps they took and the applications they made, and understand the metacognition behind the experience. Technology makes it possible to take something that was once one-dimensional, like a poster, and layer it with student voice, explanations, and even virtual reality to make their learning come to life. The result is that learning becomes much more meaningful and interesting in the process.

In the following pages, we will give you an overview of the technology tools that make it easy to allow for a variety of demonstrations of learning that are fun for the students.

In each type of demonstration of learning, students start with a question that is built around a learning target. Then students construct knowledge, keep record of their journey, and show their learning in a digitally rich product.

> "Understanding is revealed when students make sense of and transfer their learning through authentic performance."

— **McTighe and Wiggins,** *Understanding by Design*

What do you grade? You grade growth! Evaluate their *growth toward the learning target,* not the fonts they used, the number of pages, the number of questions they got right, or the mistakes they made along the way.

Strategy

FIRST, allow students the choice to respond in a way that fits their learning style. Make sure they are aware of the learning target toward which they are trying to show growth. Show them exemplars from other students if you have them— or examples you have curated from other sources.

NEXT, if it is something that fits their learning style, let them use one of the ten tools we will cover in this section. They might do a screencast, a video, or even a podcast.

FINALLY, allow them the opportunity to keep these demonstrations of learning in a portfolio where they can start to curate their learning journey. Being able to see growth over time is powerful not only to the teacher but to the student as well.

Demonstrations of Learning
STUDENT PUBLISHING
USING DIGITAL BOOKS

Demonstrations of Learning refers to a wide range of products that allow students to "demonstrate" what they have learned. These learning products provide the student the opportunity to show they have met certain learning goals or targets. If designed correctly, these demonstrations should provide the teacher with rich information about student learning and growth far beyond what can be gleaned from standard multiple choice questions or worksheets. This section provides examples of the different activities and tools students can use to show their learning.

WHY WE DO THIS: We encourage students to publish their work so that they become authors, develop their reading and writing skills, and hone their digital literacy. They do this by creating for and sharing with an authentic audience. Students can keep track of their ideas in one place, create reflection and understanding journals, and write pieces that will show their learning and growth over time. You could easily have students in any subject area and of every age publish their writing in the form of digital books.

HOW DIGITAL PUBLISHING MAKES STUDENT THINKING VISIBLE: Digital books and journals prompt students to compile the many stages of their learning in a single location. They can add graphics and videos, record and talk through their ideas and thinking using the sound function, and show their work using the drawing functions.

HOW DIGITAL PUBLISHING AMPLIFIES STUDENT VOICE: When students have a place to gather their thinking, such as in the form of a book or journal, they create a collection of work that can help them better understand who they are as a learner. What's more, as a creative tool, digital publishing gives each student a platform to develop their voice, both as a learner and a writer.

HOW DIGITAL PUBLISHING ALLOWS STUDENTS TO SHARE THEIR WORK: Students can publish their work using Book Creator or create a digital portfolio.

WHAT STUDENTS CAN CREATE: Have them make collaborative global books with schools from across the world.

YOU COULD TRY: Task them with creating science or math journals, interactive stories, digital portfolios, research journals, and science write-ups.

OR EVEN: They could develop books of sentence starters, how-to books, photo books, collaborative class anthologies focused on a unit of study, blackout poetry, and poetry journals.

AND FOR THE TEACHER: Create differentiated instructional books for your learners.

TIP: Share your students' digital books and journals through Google Classroom or your class's Google Site.

"If students are sharing their work with the world, they want it to be good. If they're just sharing it with you, they want it good enough."

– **Rushton Hurley**

4 Cs:
Critical Thinking
Communication
Collaboration
Creativity

ADVANCED:
Curation

BOOK CREATOR (Freemium)$

GOOGLE INFUSION: Book Creator and Google Drive

WHAT IS BOOK CREATOR? Book Creator is a website (BookCreator.com) and iOS app that allows students to create books, comics, journals, and authentic learning artifacts, which they can then publish online for others to view and read.

GREAT BECAUSE ... it allows students to easily publish their work.

SET UP IS ... EASY. Students simply sign in to Book Creator using their Google account.

STUDENTS TURN IN WORK BY ... publishing to your private class bookshelf within the Book Creator app or link to it in Google Classroom. They can draft the work in Google Docs and showcase the work in their own book using Book Creator. They can even upload and save in Google Drive when needed.

ALLOWS STUDENTS TO ... work independently and collaboratively to create digital books and journals.

SHOWS YOU INFORMATION IN THIS WAY ... students and teachers can view their book or journal on the Book Creator website, share it via social media, or link to it on their personal web page.

This tool works with other tools, including:

WeVideo
Screencastify
Canva

Demonstrations of Learning
VISUAL STORYTELLING 2

WHY WE DO THIS: When we ask our learners to show us what they know using a visual medium, we're asking them to research, write, think critically, and carefully organize their understanding in a coherent, meaningful way. This demonstration of learning encourages students to apply higher-order thinking skills.

HOW VISUAL STORYTELLING MAKES THINKING VISIBLE: It prompts students to tell a story through words, images, and sounds.

HOW VISUAL STORYTELLING AMPLIFIES STUDENT VOICE: Visual storytelling provides a medium through which learners can show and narrate their understanding of concepts.

HOW VISUAL STORYTELLING ALLOWS STUDENTS TO SHARE THEIR WORK: Students can publish their creations to the class blog, their digital portfolio, or a YouTube channel, then share them privately or via social media, thereby allowing an authentic audience to view their work.

WHAT STUDENTS CAN CREATE

YOU COULD TRY: Have students create documentaries based on their research, movie trailers for book reviews, vocabulary videos, how-to videos, music videos, and interviews.

OR EVEN: They could make advertisements or commercials, public service announcements, virtual field trips, and "all about me" videos.

AND FOR THE TEACHER: Publish your students' creations to your classroom's YouTube channel, or make class trailers to get your students interested in a subject before you begin the unit.

Upload an exemplar to your Drive or YouTube channel. You could also have students create tutorial videos then publish them to your class's YouTube channel.

If you teach older students, have them promote this channel and gain viewership by sharing it to social media. Your class could also have a Facebook page and class Twitter account that they share videos to as well.

"The future belongs to a different kind of person with a different kind of mind: artists, inventors, storytellers—creative and holistic 'right-brain' thinkers."

— Daniel Pink

4 Cs:
Critical Thinking
Communication
Collaboration
Creativity

ADVANCED:
Curation

WEVIDEO (Freemium)$

GOOGLE INFUSION: WeVideo and Google Drive

WHAT IS WEVIDEO? WeVideo is a web-based video creation platform.

GREAT BECAUSE ... it allows students to share their video creations with a group and edit them collaboratively.

SET UP IS ... INTERMEDIATE. You can create your student groups by inviting students manually or using a registration link or an invitation code. WeVideo's ninety-day trial period for educators provides you with 1 GB of storage, the ability to export up to five minutes of 720p video per month, and a watermark—all free of charge.

STUDENTS TURN IN WORK BY ... completing their work in the WeVideo app, then submitting it in Google Classroom, or uploading it to their Google Drive or YouTube channel (they would give you the link).

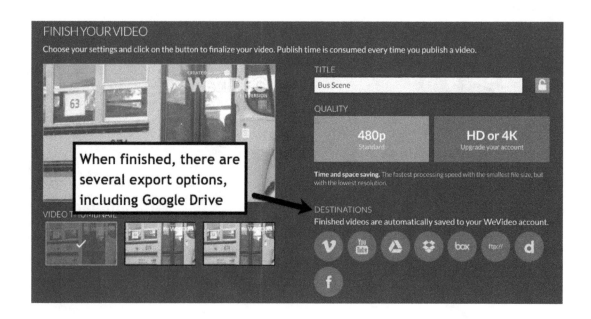

ALLOWS STUDENTS TO … create and edit videos and **screencasts**, upload media from your Google Drive, and curate playlists.

SHOWS YOU THE INFORMATION IN THIS WAY … WeVideo presents your students' work in a timeline, which you can export as a video to their Google Drive or YouTube accounts when publishing.

This tool works with other tools, including:

Canva
Screencastify
Soundtrap

Demonstrations of Learning
PODCASTING AND CREATING AUDIO AND MUSIC RECORDINGS

WHY WE DO THIS: A podcast allows students to record their voices and publish their recording for others to listen to, similar to a radio broadcast. Once they've created a podcast, they can edit, add sound effects, and share with an authentic audience. Creating podcasts helps students develop their research and writing skills, articulate their thoughts, build a diverse vocabulary, gain an audience, and learn how to promote their creations.

Additionally, music in education promotes students' creativity and free expression. When we provide an alternative outlet for students to express themselves and their understanding, we're providing them with a wider range of ways to show what they know.

HOW PODCASTING AND CREATING AUDIO AND MUSIC RECORDINGS MAKE THINKING VISIBLE: Creating recordings allows students to express their learning verbally. They can write their podcasts, edit and revise their scripts, then read and record their work. Since they can hear their thinking, they can self-edit and make necessary changes on the spot. Students can also write lyrics to songs or raps and add the pre-recorded musical instruments (loops) to demonstrate their learning.

HOW PODCASTING AND CREATING AUDIO AND MUSIC RECORDINGS AMPLIFY STUDENT VOICE: We can gain insights into our students' thinking and understanding just by listening to their recordings. If we allow them to express their learning through music, we're offering them creative freedom to express their understanding in a personally meaningful way.

HOW PODCASTING AND CREATING AUDIO AND MUSIC RECORDINGS ALLOW STUDENTS TO SHARE THEIR WORK: Students can collaborate on a podcast or music production with students in their classroom, from across the country, or around the world. They can also share their podcasts or audio and music recordings through iTunes or by posting them on your class's blog.

WHAT STUDENTS CAN CREATE: Have students record themselves reading a book on one track then create a soundtrack based on the story's theme on another track.

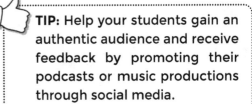

TIP: Help your students gain an authentic audience and receive feedback by promoting their podcasts or music productions through social media.

Have students create audio reflection logs on books they are reading for personal choice. Every evening, have students record a brief reflection describing what they are reading and explaining their thoughts and understanding of the book. The student creates a new voice track, placing the latest track after the previous night's recording so that they only use one track for the entire book. The student shares their reflections with the teacher to show progress in their reading comprehension.

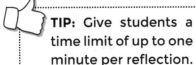

TIP: Give students a time limit of up to one minute per reflection.

Or Even: They could create and record advertisements, interviews, tutorials, stories, poetry slams, and reading fluency logs.

And Finally: Soundtrap can also serve as a tool for assessing your students' oral language skills. For example, you could task students with using Soundtrap to record their speaking all year as a single track, allowing you to see and measure their growth over time. (This method works especially well for English language learners.) Students could then put this demonstration of growth in their digital portfolio.

"You just need one person to listen, get your message, and pass it on to someone else, and you've doubled your audience."

– Robert Gerrish

4 Cs:
Critical Thinking
Communication
Collaboration
Creativity

ADVANCED:
Curation

SOUNDTRAP (Freemium)$

GOOGLE INFUSION: Soundtrap and Google Classroom

WHAT IS SOUNDTRAP? Soundtrap is a collaborative digital audio work-station that allows you and your students to create sound recordings.

GREAT BECAUSE ... students can create music and podcasts on any de-vice (Chromebooks, laptops, iPads, and smartphones) anywhere with access to the Internet. Soundtrap provides them with a bank of pre-cre-ated loops so they can develop high-quality music recordings. Students also have the ability to record their voices only.

SET UP IS ... INTERMEDIATE. Sign into Soundtrap with your Google ac-count, create your classes in the "edu admin" dashboard, then have stu-dents log in through Google Classroom, which works seamlessly with Soundtrap.

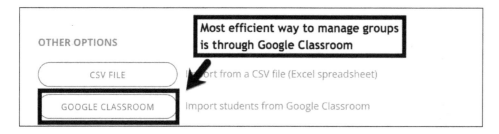

STUDENTS TURN IN WORK BY ... downloading and submitting their re-cordings as MP3 files to Classroom or sharing their creations with their teacher within the Soundtrap app.

ALLOWS YOU TO ... let students both work alone and collaborate with people from all over the world.

WHAT'S GREAT IS THAT ... it has a wide range of easy-to-use pre-re-corded loops to choose from and the ability for many students to work simultaneously on the same recording.

SHOWS YOU THE INFORMATION IN THIS WAY ... You can view work on Soundtrap in the recording 'studio' or download files as MP3s.

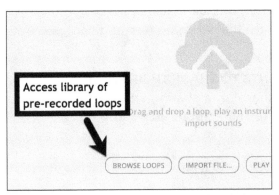

Access library of pre-recorded loops

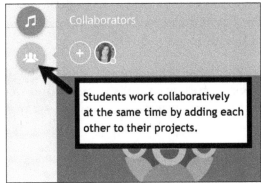

Students work collaboratively at the same time by adding each other to their projects.

This tool works with other tools, including:

WeVideo

Explain Everything

Demonstrations of Learning
THINK-PIC-SHARE AND CANVA

4

• ➤

WHY WE DO THIS: We must teach our students how to illustrate their ideas in a digital world. After all, developing visual literacy is essential to becoming digitally literate. In a "think-pic-share" students learn how to summarize and retell.

HOW USING "THINK-PIC-SHARE" MAKES THINKING VISIBLE: When implementing "think-pic-share" into your lessons, initially ask your students to **think** about and summarize what they've learned. Then have them find a **picture** that accurately represents the summary of their learning and add their thoughts in text to that graphic. Have them **share** their pic on something like a Padlet.

HOW USING "THINK-PIC-SHARE" AMPLIFIES STUDENT VOICE: When we ask our students to make a "think-pic-share," we're giving each of them a chance to create something using their own unique ideas. In making their own creative choices, they demonstrate their own understanding of the concept.

HOW "THINK-PIC-SHARE" ALLOWS STUDENTS TO SHARE THEIR WORK: Having students publish their "think-pic-share" in a sharing space like Padlet or Google Classroom allows them to think about and compare their ideas with their peers.

WHAT STUDENTS CAN CREATE:

YOU COULD TRY: Have your students write a six-word summary about what they just learned.

OR EVEN: Try doing a quick reflection with your students using Canva so they can learn thinking strategies, like the following one from *Making Thinking Visible*, by Ron Ritchhart, Mark Church and Karin Morrison.

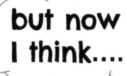

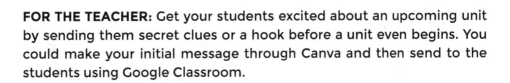

FOR THE TEACHER: Get your students excited about an upcoming unit by sending them secret clues or a hook before a unit even begins. You could make your initial message through Canva and then send to the students using Google Classroom.

> "When ideas and related concepts can be encapsulated in an image, the brain remembers the information associated with that image."
>
> – Katrina Schwartz

4 Cs:
Critical Thinking
Communication
Collaboration
Creativity

ADVANCED:
Curation

CANVA

GOOGLE INFUSION: Canva and Google Drive

WHAT IS CANVA? Canva is a free online graphic design platform that allows you and your students to quickly create professional, customized graphics. In the company's own words, it's "an amazingly simple graphic design tool."

WHAT'S GREAT IS THAT ... Canva is simple and makes it easy for students to share their work. Since they're members of Gen Z, you'll notice that your students will quickly figure out how to use this program and need very little guidance from you.

SET UP IS ... EASY. Students just sign in to Canva using their Google accounts.

STUDENTS SHOW THEIR WORK BY ... downloading their work as a PNG, JPEG, or PDF then placing it on a shareable site like Classroom or Padlet.

WHAT'S GREAT IS THAT ... it has a wide range of easy-to-use assets, icons and fonts to help students become more skilled at designing better graphics.

ALLOWS YOU TO ... have students work independently or with peers to create visual demonstrations of their learning.

SHOWS YOU THE INFORMATION IN THIS WAY ... as a graphic, but Canva features a dashboard that allows you to come back and edit your work later on, if needed, as well as download it as an image.

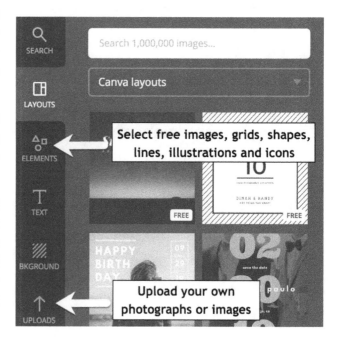

Demonstrations of Learning
SCREENCASTING

WHY WE DO THIS: Screencasting helps students capture, explain, and reflect on the work that is on their screen.

HOW SCREENCASTING MAKES THINKING VISIBLE: It allows students to add narrated explanations and reflections that better explain their learning process, to a basic document or digital artifact (like a poster). To do this, students simply show the artifact on the screen and record their thinking. You could then use these recordings to see if your students demonstrate their understanding of the learning targets.

HOW SCREENCASTING AMPLIFIES STUDENT VOICE: It gives all students a chance to explain their understanding and thinking using a tool other than the written word.

HOW SCREENCASTING ALLOWS STUDENTS TO SHARE THEIR WORK: Screencasting gives your students the opportunity to provide you and their parents with a more in-depth understanding of where they are in their learning process, as well as to receive feedback from others.

WHAT STUDENTS CAN CREATE: Consider having them make **video reflective journals**, explanations of their writing using a document's revision history, a story arc and talk-through (place a story arc on screen then talk through ideas for its plot and character development before starting the writing process), and narrated demonstrations of mathematical problem solving.

YOU COULD TRY: Have students hone their accent and conversational skills in a foreign language by reading and speaking in that language, add narration to their video slideshow and present it to you instead of the entire class, and create animations using Google Draw and its revision history.

OR EVEN: Let students make tutorials and dedicate an entire YouTube channel to your class's tutorials.

AND FOR THE TEACHER: Clone yourself and leave directions for your students by creating differentiated tutorial videos for when you're home sick or at a conference.

"Most of all, have the confidence in every learner's ability to think and your capacity to nurture that thinking. The results will amaze and energize you."

–Ron Ritchhart, Mark Church, and Karin Morrison from *Making Thinking Visible*

4 Cs:
Critical Thinking
Communication
Collaboration
Creativity

ADVANCED:
Curation

SCREENCASTIFY

GOOGLE INFUSION: Screencastify and Google Drive

WHAT IS SCREENCASTIFY? Screencastify is a Google Chrome Extension that allows you and your students to capture and record all of the screen activity that takes place within a tab, including audio.

GREAT BECAUSE ... You can record everything on your screen, with or without a webcam.

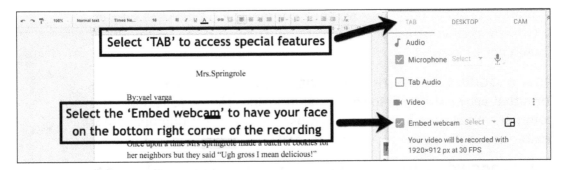

SET UP IS ... EASY. Once you've installed the app, just click on the Extension and choose if you want to record your entire screen, only your face, or your screen with your face visible on the bottom-right corner.

STUDENTS TURN IN WORK BY ... submitting their work to you through Classroom, Drive, Slides (embedded in the slideshow), and YouTube.

ALLOWS STUDENTS TO ... capture and share their thought processes behind and reflections on their work and creations.

SHOWS THE INFORMATION TO YOU IN THIS WAY ... Screencastify presents work as videos.

This tool works with other tools, including 'A Web Whiteboard' (AWW);

Google Docs
Slides and Draw
YouTube

Demonstrations of Learning
BLOGGING

WHY WE DO THIS: Blogging gives students an opportunity to speak to a real, authentic audience, as well as reflect on and journal their learning. Encourage students to use their blog's analytics of site visits to gain a better understanding of what makes a good post, then use that information to continually improve their content. Blog posts are typically written in an informal or conversational style, and the writing itself should not be graded.

HOW BLOGGING MAKES THINKING VISIBLE: Blogs are a versatile platform that allows students to show their thinking, create, reflect on, and comment on almost any topic in almost any class, including, but not limited to, English, science, math, P.E., and foreign languages.

HOW BLOGGING AMPLIFIES STUDENT VOICE: A blog provides students with a forum where they can develop ideas and cultivate their academic identity, while at the same time allowing the teacher to assess their path toward growth. As an added bonus, you'll find that your introverted students will often share more online than they do in person or during class.

HOW BLOGGING ALLOWS STUDENTS TO SHARE THEIR WORK: When students write and publish blog posts, they can share them with you and their classmates—and better yet, the world. This gives them the opportunity to begin building an audience for their work and learn how to use analytics to determine what makes good content. If there are many visits to a particular post, students can deconstruct or analyze why this particular content resonated with a larger audience. This critical thinking can be an important skill they will likely need in their future careers, as it will help them to create writing and artifacts that are of higher interest.

WHAT STUDENTS CAN CREATE: Task them with making **learning journals** and diaries; how-to blogs; lists (for example, "10 Things You Need to Know About Quadratic Equations"); "vlogs" (video blogs); podcasts (see page 56); and digital portfolios of growth.

YOU COULD TRY: They could create a book reviews website; a class news blog (replacing the class newsletter); student note-takers blogs (where students post their class notes); and quick reflections.

OR EVEN: Have students attempt the **100-Word Challenge** and Quad-Blogging.

A note on commenting: Students can and should comment on one another's blog posts in a way that helps the writer grow as a learner; however, teaching students to effectively comment requires some work on the front end. You can accomplish this through lessons around the foundations of appropriate commenting, as well as how to comment in a way that provides valuable feedback for the person or readers.

AND FOR THE TEACHER: You may want to maintain a class blog, populating it with everything from great examples of student work to a preview of upcoming homework. You could also create blogs for your school's clubs, student groups, events, and sports teams, as well as pose questions and receive responses from around the world. Broaden your blog's audience by sharing it through Twitter and Pinterest.

"Blogs are whatever we make them. Defining 'blog' is a fool's errand."

– Jeff Jarvis

4 Cs:
Critical Thinking
Communication
Collaboration
Creativity

ADVANCED:
Curation

BLOGGER

GOOGLE INFUSION: Blogger and Google Drive

WHAT IS BLOGGER? Blogger is a Google-owned blogging platform that you and your students can use to regularly update a learning log, class journal, or website.

GREAT BECAUSE ... Students can easily publish their work or keep a journal of their learning. Students can also use the site analytics to see which posts are most popular or attracted the biggest audience. This will help them think critically about content, and how what they produce affects their ability to be a global contributor.

+5	0 💬	789 👁	2/24/17
	0 💬	241 👁	2/23/17
+10	0 💬	954 👁	2/22/17

SET UP IS ... EASY. Just choose one of Blogger's templates and start writing and posting. The platform's difficulty level increases as you personalize your blog.

ALLOWS STUDENTS TO ... stay organized and keep track of their learning and ideas in one location.

GIVES YOU THIS INFORMATION ... posts are listed as a chronological log. You can also take advantage of the platform's navigational tools.

WHAT'S GREAT IS THAT ... it allows you to quickly and easily reach a global audience.

SHOWS YOU THE INFORMATION IN THIS WAY ... Blogger lists the posts chronologically, with the oldest ones at the bottom. Students can set up a more complicated navigation structure based on a tool-based skill level.

OR YOU CAN TRY...SEESAW!

GOOGLE INFUSION: Seesaw sites and Google Drive

WHAT IS SEESAW? Seesaw is a digital portfolio app and website that can be a powerful tool for making student thinking visible. Seesaw also has a blog option that students can use to publish their creations to an authentic audience.

GREAT BECAUSE ... It provides students with multiple ways to document their learning. Students can easily create videos, photos, and voice recordings. They may even add a QR code to their creation, print it, and post it in your class so their peers can scan the code and listen to their recording and provide comments—something like a gallery walk. Once shared on the blog option, their creation can be made public to a larger audience.

SET UP IS ... EASY. Create your classes, add your students, then provide them with either a QR code or class code so they can enter your class. Set up a blog by selecting the globe icon on the right corner of the page. You will be provided with a URL that can be shared so pre-approved student posts become public.

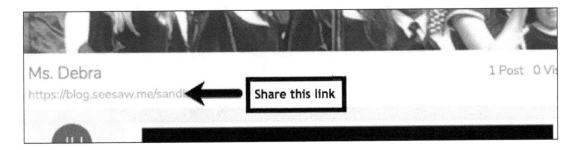

STUDENTS TURN IN WORK BY ... adding responses and then selecting the green checkmark on the top-right corner of the screen. They can organize their work by using folders if the teacher makes them in advance. The teacher then has the option to publish students' work onto the blog.

ALLOWS STUDENTS TO …

1. take pictures of their "analog" creations where they can add drawings, add text, and record their voice to provide insight on their process;

2. create a video recording within the app;

3. add a written note;

4. add voice, draw on, or add text to a picture that is already saved on the device, insert a picture or video that was created in another app or saved on your desktop or Google Drive;

5. insert a file (i.e., Doc, Slides, Drawing, Sheets) from Google Drive that will be converted as a PDF on Seesaw. Students can add audio annotation or write a text caption.

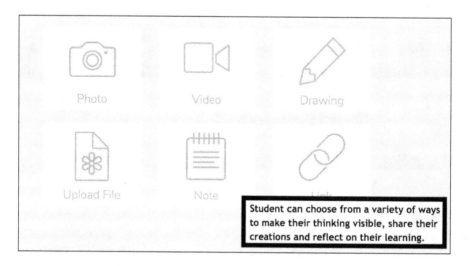

Student can choose from a variety of ways to make their thinking visible, share their creations and reflect on their learning.

SHOWS YOU INFORMATION THIS WAY … on individual feeds, creating a chronological record of their reflections. Using the calendar feature, you can view the work of the entire class or individual student arranged by chronological date or on the public blog.

Demonstrations of Learning
COLLABORATIVE STUDENT CREATIONS *WITH SLIDES*

WHY WE DO THIS: Collaborative tools give students the opportunity to work on a platform that is easy to utilize, edit, and share with others.

HOW COLLABORATIVE STUDENT CREATIONS MAKE THINKING VISIBLE: These projects provide students an opportunity to show and reflect on their learning while working with and receiving feedback from their peers.

HOW COLLABORATIVE STUDENT CREATIONS AMPLIFY STUDENT VOICE: They give each student a space in which to develop and share their ideas. Students can then add to their peers' work, amplifying the class's overall learning.

HOW COLLABORATIVE STUDENT CREATIONS ALLOW STUDENTS TO SHARE THEIR WORK: Students can share their creations with each other and work on the overall product together. When they are done, they can publish their creations to the web and share with others, providing them with opportunities to receive invaluable feedback on their creations from their peers or outside experts.

TIP: To teach digital literacy, point students toward social media so they can gather an even more dynamic audience and gain responses and perspectives from around the world..

WHAT STUDENTS CAN CREATE: Of course, they can make collaborative presentations, but let's go further than that and be more creative.

YOU COULD TRY:

SIX-WORD SUMMARIES—Students do a six-word summary of an event or a chapter, then share it with the class using Slides.

100-WORD CHALLENGE—Students collaborate on the weekly writing prompt using a shared Slides presentation.

NON-DIGITAL CREATIONS—in Google Slides, students can go to *insert* and choose image. From there they can select take a Snapshot, which allows them to use their webcam to take a picture of something they are working on or have completed.

CLICK 'N' LISTENS—To convey student thinking in a fun, creative way, have students choose a bitmoji that represents an idea, emotion, or anything else they want to communicate. They can then use the Google Chrome extension Talk and Comment to record themselves giving an explanation. They then take the link provided by Talk and Comment and add it as a hyperlink to the bitmoji (or any image).

"THINK-PIC-SHARE"—Students find a graphic that represents a quote or an idea from their learning then put text at the top of the graphic, creating a "think-pic-share."

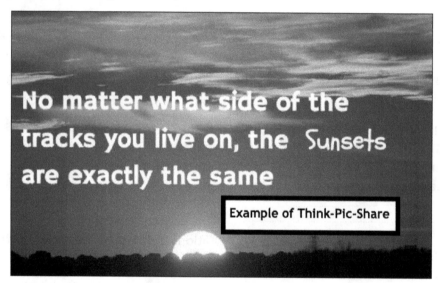

Example of Think-Pic-Share

USE TEMPLATES—Using a creative template like a fake Instagram feed, have students create profiles for characters from the lesson or even personifications of science and math concepts.

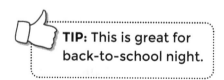

TIP: This is great for back-to-school night.

OR EVEN:

CREATION GALLERIES—So that everyone can see one another's creations, have students put their work in a slideshow, creating a gallery. This can be done to showcase each individual student's creations or to share collaboratively in one slide deck.

AND FOR THE TEACHER: Explain your directions and learning targets in Slides then record the presentation using Screencastify.

POLL EVERYWHERE—Install the Poll Everywhere Slides Extension and ask students to answer questions or plot their ideas on a chart.

"Alone we can
do so little;
together we can
do so much."

—Helen Keller

4 Cs:
Critical Thinking
Communication
Collaboration
Creativity

ADVANCED:
Curation

GOOGLE SLIDES

GOOGLE INFUSION: Screencastify and Google Drive

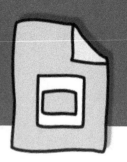

WHAT IS GOOGLE SLIDES? Google Slides is an online collaborative and visual space that most people think about as a presentation platform, but it is *so* much more! It allows students to create demonstrations of learning that they are able to share with an audience outside of the physical walls of their classroom.

GREAT BECAUSE ... Slides lets you go beyond text and adding pictures. Students can bring in drawings, equations, images, and videos. They can use voice typing, and if they are advanced they can make amazing animations!

SET UP IS ... EASY. Once you are on your Drive, click the blue "NEW" button and choose "Google Slides."

Tip: Type in slides.google.com

STUDENTS TURN IN BY ... Google Classroom or Drive account or share it with you as a link.

ALLOWS STUDENTS TO ... edit the same presentation file simultaneously with their peers and share their work on the web.

SHOWS YOU THE INFORMATION IN THIS WAY ... The presentation platform creates one document that you can easily access, navigate, and use to check students' understanding and evaluate intended learning outcomes.

This tool works with other tools, including:

YouTube
Google Sites
Google Classroom
Screencastify

Demonstrations of Learning
COLLABORATIVE WRITING

WHY WE DO THIS: Collaborative writing allows students to work with others to expand upon their ideas and amplify the writing process.

HOW COLLABORATIVE WRITING MAKES THINKING VISIBLE: When students work together they must be able to explain their thoughts and ideas to each other. Google Docs allows for this through the commenting feature. This is expanded upon when students use the Talk and Comment extension to leave audio comments for their collaborators.

HOW COLLABORATIVE WRITING AMPLIFIES STUDENT VOICE: Even students who are slow to write can often produce more written material when they are working as a pair. Being able to collaborate allows students to come up with more ideas and filter these through the lens of another perspective.

HOW COLLABORATIVE WRITING ALLOWS STUDENTS TO SHARE THEIR WORK: Students begin by sharing first with their collaboration partner and later, if they chose, with a larger audience by going to *File* and then choosing to publish to the web, Google Classroom, or Google Sites.

WHAT STUDENTS CAN CREATE: Your students can make documents, drawings, tables, journals, and reading PDFs.

> **VOICE TYPING (SPEECH TO TEXT)**—This is a tool provided in Google Docs via the Tools section. Students who cannot yet type or whom you think may fare better speaking their ideas before writing them down will like this feature.

> **VOICE COMMENTING (THE TALK AND COMMENT EXTENSION)**—Use this tool to leave verbal comments for those students who do better with auditory instructions. You could also have students record themselves reading their work aloud or leave audio notes as they write.

READING FLUENCY JOURNALS—Ask students to read aloud a PDF uploaded to Docs, then have them capture their reading fluency using Screencastify to share with you and include in their portfolio.

Revision History—When students are collaborating on a document, it can be quite informative to use the Revision History feature (under the File menu.) Here you can see, through "show changes," how often each student actually contributed to the final product.

YOU COULD TRY: Have students do a collaborative writing assignment with at least two classmates. Here they can jump into the same document using the 'share document' feature, making sure both parties have editing access rights.

OR EVEN: Upload a short story in PDF form. Have students explain their thinking at certain points in the story using the "comments" feature—this feature makes student comments similar to the idea of writing in the margins.

AND FOR THE TEACHER: (HyperDocs. See Page 44.)

> "The fun for me in collaboration is, one, working with other people just makes you smarter; that's proven."
>
> —Lin-Manuel Miranda

4 Cs:
Critical Thinking
Communication
Collaboration
Creativity

ADVANCED:
Curation

GOOGLE DOCS

GOOGLE INFUSION: Google Docs and Google Classroom

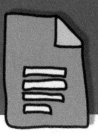

WHAT ARE GOOGLE DOCS? In the past, writing was an isolated activity; but now, thanks to Google Docs, multiple students can easily edit, comment on, and view a single document at the same time.

GREAT BECAUSE ... a Doc lives in the cloud and is accessible from any device. It can also be shared with anyone, from any continent, at any time, making it the perfect way to have students in different locations collaborate.

SET UP IS ... EASY. Just go to your Google Drive, press the blue "NEW" button, and choose "Google Docs."

Tip: Type in docs.google.com

STUDENTS TURN IN BY ... sharing a doc with you through Classroom or Drive. They can also share a direct link to the document.

ALLOWS STUDENTS TO ... easily collaborate. In the process of working together they can help each other edit by using suggested edits and commenting features.

SHOWS YOU THE INFORMATION IN THIS WAY... in text format, but graphics and images can easily be added

This tool works with other tools, including Google Draw, Screencastify, Google Classroom, and Talk and Comment.

This tool works with other tools, including:

Google Draw

Screencastify

Google Classroom

Talk and Comment

Demonstrations of Learning
COLLABORATIVE INTERACTIVE WHITEBOARD

WHY WE DO THIS: Collaborative interactive whiteboards help students capture, explain, and reflect on their learning, using a more powerful platform that allows for animation, compare and contrast, movie making, and **sketchnoting**. Basically anything your students need to do can be done in a collaborative shared whiteboard, the best one being Explain Everything.

HOW COLLABORATIVE INTERACTIVE WHITEBOARDS MAKES THINKING VISIBLE: It allows students to demonstrate their understanding and their thinking process. Students are able show their work on the screen while recording themselves telling us what they are thinking, what steps they took, and their thought process behind the work.

HOW COLLABORATIVE INTERACTIVE WHITEBOARDS AMPLIFY STUDENT VOICE: It gives them a place to express their learning in their own creative way, with a more powerful set of tools and functions. With these enhanced features, their ability to share what they have learned is amplified.

HOW COLLABORATIVE INTERACTIVE WHITEBOARDS ALLOW STUDENTS TO SHARE THEIR WORK: Students can publish their creations to share with the class or with a global audience. They can even share with another student and work on the creation together in real time.

WHAT STUDENTS CAN CREATE

TUTORIALS—Students can create tutorials of math, a foreign language, or any concept taught in class. They can then use the videos to teach one another or curate a help channel for students in younger grades. The best videos can also be used to help differentiate instruction for other students in the class.

COMPARE AND CONTRAST VIDEO—Have students curate two different videos of a similar event, like a time lapse of a science experiment. Then capture their understanding of why they turned out differently using the record feature, with reflections and real scientific reasoning.

SKETCHNOTING WITH VOICEOVERS—This is great for visual learners. Students sketch out their notes and ideas using mind mapping or **sketchnoting** techniques then narrate that thinking process using the record feature.

CHECK FOR FLUENCY AND COMPREHENSION—Have students upload a story into Explain Everything, then use the recording tool to record themselves reading the piece. They can use the pointer tool to help them progress along the screen. At the end of the fluency recording, have them provide a brief summary of what happened and discuss any subtextual information that they might have found interesting. There you have captured their fluency and comprehension and can use this to chart their growth throughout the school year by doing this once a month.

INTERACTIVE TIMELINES—Have students use Explain Everything to place historical events in chronological order using text and images, then recording their voice and explanations.

OR EVEN:

BLACKOUT POETRY: Have students takes a black marker tool to uploaded poems, newspapers, or stories (anything text based) and begin redacting words until a poem is formed.

WHITEBOARD ANIMATION—This is a process where a story is told with pictures. The images are drawn on a digital whiteboard by students who record themselves telling the story as the pictures appear and disappear. For a good example, see Ken Robinson's Ted Talk done by RSA Animate on bit.ly/ExampleVideos.

TRIPS TO FOREIGN COUNTRIES—Foreign language students can put together a virtual trip to a famous city, then narrate the trip in the foreign language to help them practice conversational speech and authentic accents.

LETTER AND LETTER SOUNDS TREASURE HUNT—Students must explore their class and school to look for examples of beginning letter sounds and/or images of objects that begin with that letter. Students then create a screencast of the treasure hunt explaining their discoveries.

AND FOR THE TEACHER:

Create an On-Demand Resource—Use Explain Everything instead of a SMART or Promethean board as a primary tool for direct instruction. As the teacher gives a live lesson, they can record the lesson and explanations that are being projected onto their screen using Explain Everything. Once the instruction is done, there is a recording that can be shared later with students as an on-demand resource. This is a great way to create a bank of curated, differentiated video tutorials for students.

GRADE A PAPER—Bring in a paper to Explain Everything and use the tools and record feature to show students places where they might improve or expand on their ideas. When finished, share the explanation with the student.

> "Technology is used to strengthen teacher-student relationships and interactions around learning, and not replace the relationships or interactions."
>
> —**Reshan Richards**

4 Cs:
Critical Thinking
Communication
Collaboration
Creativity

ADVANCED:
Curation

EXPLAIN EVERYTHING

GOOGLE INFUSION: Explain Everything and Google Drive

WHAT IS EXPLAIN EVERTHING? Explain Everything is a collaborative on-line whiteboard that allows students to draw and create content, import most file formats, record everything happening on your screen with narration, and export anywhere.

GREAT BECAUSE...students can create animations, movies, and tutorials. They can take text-based and visual notes (sketchnotes), all in one application.

SET UP IS... EASY. Start by using it as a whiteboard. It becomes more intermediate when you begin to add visuals and use the bank of design tools to create interactive visuals and lessons.

ALLOWS STUDENTS TO ... import and export almost any file content—image, document, video, website, equations, and more—to and from almost anywhere.

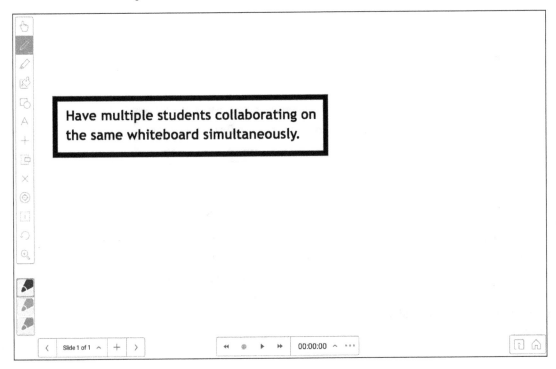

Have multiple students collaborating on the same whiteboard simultaneously.

GIVES YOU THIS INFORMATION ... You can view and save content as a movie, PDF, image, or editable project file.

STUDENTS TURN IN BY ... an upload to Drive or host on Explain Everything Discover, an online sharing community.

SHOWS YOU THE INFORMATION IN THIS WAY... as a video or image.

This tool works with other tools, including Google Drive, Classroom, Sites, Slides, Docs.

COST: Yearly Subscription ($2.67 per EDU user per year)

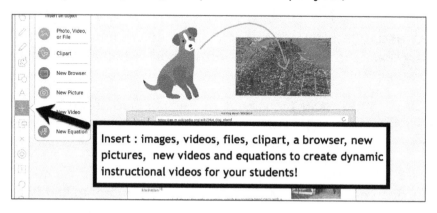

Insert : images, videos, files, clipart, a browser, new pictures, new videos and equations to create dynamic instructional videos for your students!

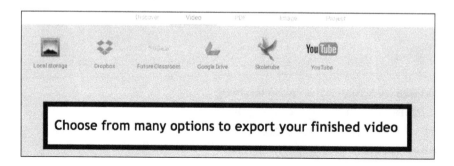

Choose from many options to export your finished video

As our students create artifacts of learning, they need to have a place to curate and reflect on their learning experiences. The next section explores reflection as it is used to demonstrate student learning and growth. We will examine some of the best tools that can be used for reflection and to help students make their thinking visible, amplify their voice, and share their creations with an authentic audience.

Formative Assessment

Tips for Differentiation

Demonstrations of Learning

Reflection and Curation

Reflection and Curation
AND THE TOOLS TO USE

As educators, our job is to help students make meaning of concepts and ideas. We want them to construct knowledge and be creators of their learning, not just consumers that parrot information back to us. Ultimately, we want the experiences in our classroom to inspire curiosity and a love of learning that will last a lifetime.

Reflection is a practice that is essential for every learner-centered classroom. But the truth is that this step of the learning process often gets omitted. This omission happens for three main reasons: First, it is admittedly not an easy practice to master. And because students are so infrequently asked to reflect on their learning, they have trouble doing it well. Second, most teachers have not been taught to academically reflect, and thus don't know where to begin teaching the process with their own students. And third, it takes time. Reflection is a step that is easy to skip when teachers are already rushing to cover content in their overcrowded curriculum.

We want to encourage you to be intentional about incorporating this valuable practice in your classroom. We know this may be a new skill and that it will take some learning on your part, but think of it as an educational adventure! When you see how much reflection helps your students understand (1) the content, (2) who they are as learners, and (3) how they can apply their knowledge to future learning, you will be hooked. For us, it has been an adventure not unlike owning a puppy: You can't believe how much work it is, but when that puppy matures, it becomes your best friend.

> "We do not learn from experience ... we learn from reflecting on experience."
>
> — **John Dewey**

As educators, we must teach students how to reflect. They need to understand that, in all learning, there should be a specific time devoted to pausing and looking back at the journey and considering how they arrived at true academic knowledge. This time of self-evaluation and reflection happens when students comment on, connect with, and reassess the learning process. This is assessment *as* learning, and it is often as important to student learning and growth as the content itself.

A reflective classroom includes both oral- and text-based reflections. It is grounded in questions and routines. You might have specific questions students learn to ask, or you might use a scaffolded approach that starts out easy and moves its way to much deeper internal reflections. The end goal is to have students develop their own reflective practice. After all, the skill of reflection is a transformational life skill. Imagine a world where people critically reflected on the decisions they made and thoughtfully looked for ways they might do better next time. With that scenario in mind, which seems like a more important skill to teach students: reflection or the date of a battle in America's Civil War?

In this section, we will share a few technology tools that will allow for a rich, reflective process by students. These tools allow students to record their thinking, show their learning, and expound critically about the process.

Here are four easy ways for students to get started practicing the skill of reflection:

1) Keep a Journal or Diary

Using an app like ReCap or SeeSaw, students can keep a written diary or video journal where they list three ways they learned that day or week. This helps students develop their vocabulary around how they learn and helps them uncover their learning preferences.

For example, students might write or record the following, giving details after each comment:

I learned through prediction.

I learned through context clues.

I learned through talking with my neighbor.

2) Write a Letter

Students can use SeeSaw or Google Docs to write a short letter to themselves. In the letter, they explain their learning process and the steps they took. They tell themselves how they could apply this learning in the real world.

3) Offer Some Advice

Using Padlet or SeeSaw, students could leave advice for themselves for their next unit. For example, they might offer recommendations on what they could do differently, discuss learning patterns, expound on strengths, and talk about how they might approach the next unit of study intentionally.

For younger students, sentence stems might be a good place to start. For example, students might write or use the record feature in a SeeSaw journal to explain the following thoughts:

- I was good at...
- I liked...
- I had problems with...
- Next time I might...

4) Create a Video Reflection

Students can use Screencastify or Flipgrid to record themselves explaining their learning and uncovering their thinking process using video reflections.

No matter where you begin or how you develop a rich, reflective program, it is a very important step in any learning scenario. More importantly, students should share these reflections with each other so they can build a bigger repertoire and toolkit of reflective practices. This should be an ongoing process that becomes more detailed over time.

Strategy

FIRST, during the learning process and as you begin to wrap up a unit, decide how you'd like for your students to reflect, and then have them gather information on how they met their learning targets. You may begin the thought process by providing them with a scaffolded guiding question.

 TIP: Check out this amazing resource for thinking strategy prompts: bit.ly/GICThinking.

NEXT, choose a tool that will both assist students as they reflect on their learning journey and encourage the depth of thinking for which you're looking. Go with an easy-to-use platform for the reflection piece. We shouldn't grade reflections, as grading them will only cause students not to be as critical or honest.

FINALLY, respond to your students' reflections so they know their ideas were heard, even though you didn't grade them. Use the data you gather from the students' work to further reflect on your own practices, and adjust the unit.

 TIP: Make sure to schedule time in your lesson for students to create their reflections. If you don't intentionally do this, the reflections will most likely not happen. In addition, allow students to model their reflective experiences with each other.

Tools:

Flipgrid

Screencastify

Padlet

Seesaw

Recap

FLIPGRID

GOOGLE INFUSION: Flipgrid and Google Classroom

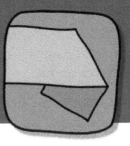

WHAT IS FLIPGRID? Flipgrid is a video-response platform featuring grids and topics. Think of it as a grid that helps you flip your instruction, hence the name Flipgrid! On a grid, you can have topics. Topics are unlimited and allow you to ask different discussion questions or prompts based on the overarching subject of the grid.

GREAT BECAUSE ... The grid environment empowers students to watch and respond to their classmates' videos as well as self-reflect. Even the students who are shy or slow to respond—the students who don't typically raise their hands—have the chance to participate with Flipgrid. It works great for students who just need a bit more time to process before they post. It also allows students to build articulate verbal reasoning skills as they post and respond. Video responses often prompt further discussions among students and the class.

SET UP IS ... EASY. You just name a grid, ask a question and let the video reflections begin. Each grid can have limitless topics - For example, name a grid "The Outsiders", and have many topics or discussions within that one grid.

ALLOWS STUDENTS TO ... watch other student videos, self-reflect, learn from each other, and compare their learning with that of their peers. This allows them to "think about thinking" and naturally throws them into a state of metacognition.

GIVES YOU INFORMATION IN THIS WAY ... Flipgrid lets your students create video responses that can lead to class discussions and puts them on one easy to navigate grid.

WHAT'S GREAT IS THAT ...It also teaches the digital citizenship lessons of commenting and communicating effectively with others via video and media. (Note: teachers need to spend a bit of time talking about proper commenting and meaningful replies first. Students don't naturally know how to do this in a constructive way. Students spend their lives taking videos, selfies and interacting on social media with a global audience. Now teachers can harness the power and fun of social media in their classrooms.

SHOWS YOU THE INFORMATION IN THIS WAY ... Everything is presented in an organized grid, which makes it highly visual, easy to navigate, and easy to assess.

A FEW EXAMPLES ...

END OF THE UNIT THINKING ROUTINE—Use the powerful thinking routine "I used to think, now I think" to have students reflect on their learning at the end of a unit.

SCIENCE—Have students take time-lapse videos of science projects and upload those to a grid. They can use the comment feature to explain what happened during the process and briefly analyze the results.

ART—Have students give their interpretations of an art piece. Then have them listen to the others' interpretations, reflecting on why they might be dramatically different.

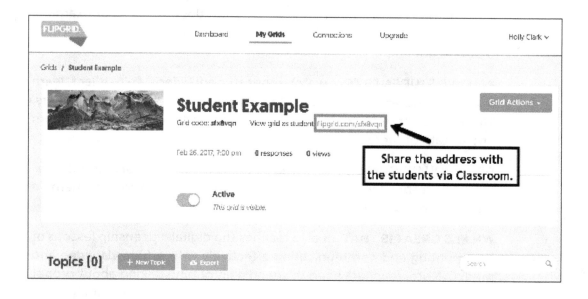

Share the address with the students via Classroom.

SCREENCASTIFY

GOOGLE INFUSION: Screencastify and Google Drive

WHAT IS SCREENCASTIFY? Screencastify is a Chrome extension that captures and records all of the screen activity within a tab, including its audio.

GREAT BECAUSE ... Students can open a Doc or learning artifact, then talk through their learning using Screencastify's tools.

SETUP IS ... EASY. Just click the Screencastify icon in your Chrome Browser and you and your students can begin recording over Google Slides, Docs, or whatever else is on the screen. Make sure to visit the Chrome Webstore to install the extension first.

ALLOWS STUDENTS TO ... display a learning artifact on their screen and record themselves talking through the learning process. If students select the tab record feature, a set of tools will appear in the bottom left corner of the screen. These tools can be used to annotate what is on the screen, which might allow students to further explain their learning process.

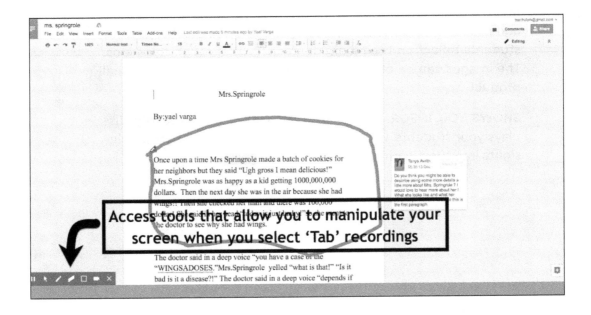

Access tools that allow you to manipulate your screen when you select 'Tab' recordings

GIVES YOU THIS INFORMATION ... Screencastify gives students the opportunity to provide verbal feedback and demonstrate an understanding of their learning (which could be used for parent-teacher conferences).

WHAT'S GREAT IS THAT ... students can turn in their screencasts using Classroom, save them to Drive to place in a digital portfolio, or upload them to their YouTube channel.

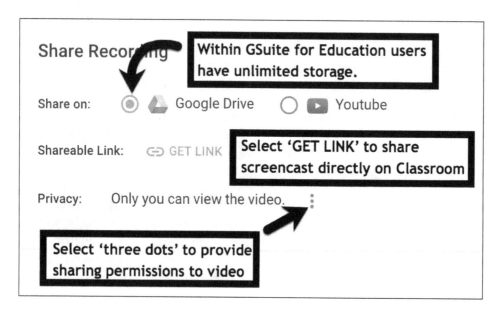

 Make thinking visible! Using slides, have students insert an image of their work to form a slideshow. Use Screencastify to have students reflect on their learning as they go through the slides. The images can be of the process of the creation or of the final product.

SHOWS YOU INFORMATION IN THIS WAY ... Screencastify displays your students' work as a video, complete with narrated insights into their learning.

PADLET

GOOGLE INFUSION: Padlet and Google Classroom

WHAT IS PADLET? Padlet is both a website and a Chrome extension that allows you to create a blank digital wall.

GREAT BECAUSE ... it's simple to use. When you don't have time for your students to make in-depth reflections, they can still use Padlet to create short text- or image-based ones.

SET UP IS ... EASY. In most cases, though, you should have Padlet ready to go before class. Go to padlet.com and sign in using your Google account. In the upper right hand corner select the Add New button, then select from Wall, Canvas, Stream, Grid, or Shelf.

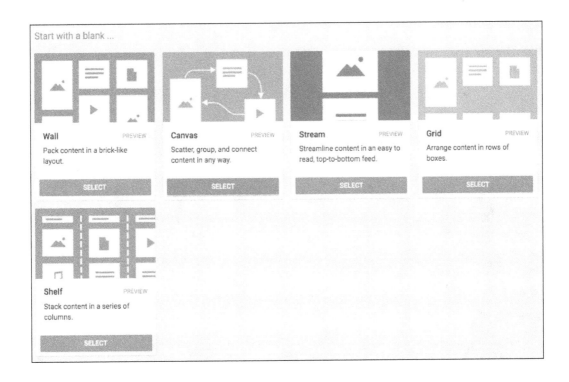

Start with a blank ...

Wall   PREVIEW
Pack content in a brick-like layout.
SELECT

Canvas   PREVIEW
Scatter, group, and connect content in any way.
SELECT

Stream   PREVIEW
Streamline content in an easy to read, top-to-bottom feed.
SELECT

Grid   PREVIEW
Arrange content in rows of boxes.
SELECT

Shelf   PREVIEW
Stack content in a series of columns.
SELECT

ALLOWS STUDENTS TO … quickly reflect on some part of the learning process by answering either a prompt or guiding question that you provide. It can also be used as a space for students to post their own reflections as they progress through a unit.

GIVES YOU THIS INFORMATION … The platform displays students' work (videos, images, and text) on a digital wall, which you can view in a wall, canvas, stream, grid, or shelf format.

Going on a Field Trip? Have students post videos and/or pictures with a reflection of their experience that day on a shared Padlet.

Teach Art? Have students create their own Padlet that they use as a gallery of their creations. Under each inserted photo, they can write reflections about their learning journey.

WHAT'S GREAT IS THAT … students can learn from one another when they see the responses from their classmates. They might learn from their peers in another class or their school or across the globe. This can also serve as a great starting place for a larger class discussion surrounding final responses.

SHOWS YOU THE INFORMATION IN THIS WAY … Padlet displays student work in a visually appealing way, much like a digital bulletin board.

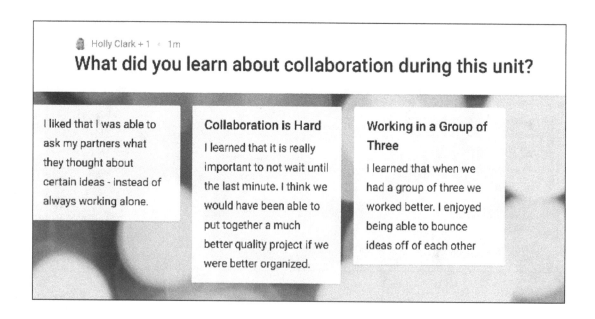

SEESAW

GOOGLE INFUSION: Seesaw and Google Drive

WHAT IS SEESAW? Seesaw is a digital portfolio app and website that can be a powerful tool for student reflection. We consider SeeSaw a making-thinking-visible *power tool*!

GREAT BECAUSE … It provides students with a way to document their learning. They can add both verbal and graphical reflections using videos, photos, and voice recordings. Students can also publish their reflections to your class blog; they may even add a QR code to their reflection, print it, and post it in your class so their peers can scan the code and listen to their recording.

SET UP IS … EASY. Create your classes, add your students, then provide them with either a QR code or class code so they can enter your class.

STUDENTS TURN IN WORK BY … adding responses and then selecting the green checkmark on the top-right corner of the screen. They can organize their work by using folders if the teacher makes them in advance.

ALLOWS STUDENTS TO …

1. take pictures of their "analog" creations where they can add drawings, add text, and record their voice to provide insight on their process;

2. create a video recording within the app;

3. add a written note;

4. add voice, draw on or add text to a picture that is already saved on the device, or insert a picture or video that was created in another app or saved on your desktop or Google Drive;

5. insert a file (i.e., Doc, Slides, Drawing, Sheets) from Google Drive that will be converted as a PDF on Seesaw. Students can add audio annotation or write a text caption.

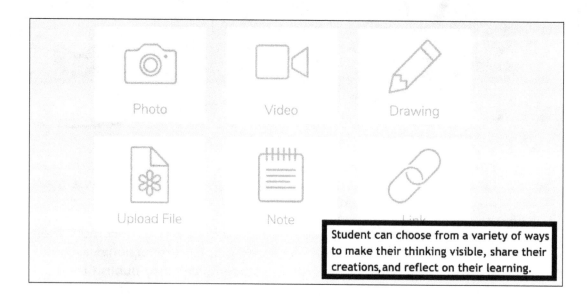

Student can choose from a variety of ways to make their thinking visible, share their creations, and reflect on their learning.

SHOWS YOU INFORMATION THIS WAY ... on individual feeds, creating a chronological record of their reflections. Using the calendar feature, you can view the work of the entire class or individual students arranged by chronological date.

Teaching Math? At the end of a unit or lesson, have students take a picture of an angle and use the drawing tool to identify the type of angle in the photo. Use the record feature to reflect on their learning around angles.

Teaching Language Arts? Have students take pictures of their favorite quotes from a book. Use the record feature to have the students explain how this quote was essential in helping them understand the meaning of the book. They can use this thinking strategy and expand on it to write a response to literature when appropriate.

RECAP

GOOGLE INFUSION: Recap and Google Classroom

WHAT IS RECAP? Recap is an app that encourages students to verbalize their thoughts and more deeply reflect on their learning by regularly creating video reflections using teacher-provided questions as prompts.

GREAT BECAUSE … you can determine how long each student's recording should last (Recap offers four options, all two minutes or less). You ask a set of questions, one right after the other, so as to reveal their thinking and understanding.

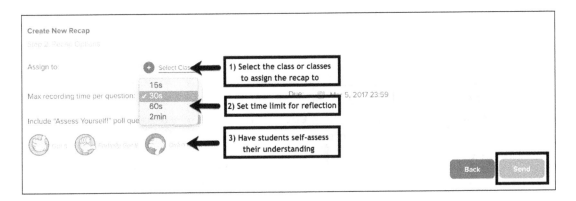

SET UP IS … EASY. Click "Add Recap," ask a question or prompt, assign a due date, select the recording's length, and decide whether your entire class or individual students should receive the task.

STUDENTS TURN WORK IN BY … using their **webcam** and microphone to record (and re-record, if needed) a video response, then submit their work. In addition, they might download it and turn it in using Google Classroom.

ALLOWS STUDENTS TO … learn how to succinctly describe where they are in their learning process using video.

GIVES YOU THIS INFORMATION … You can opt to view all of your students' reflections as one daily review reel, complete with fun animations and music, or each reflection individually (go to "View Details").

Digital Portfolios
CURATION OF LEARNING

WHY WE DO THIS: As father of experiential learning John Dewey stated, "We do not learn from experience, we learn from reflecting on experience." With this in mind, it is imperative that students curate, archive, and build upon their classwork. A digital portfolio becomes the place for reflection as part of the "for" and "as" assessment pieces (discussed in detail on Page 26).

HOW DIGITAL PORTFOLIOS MAKE THINKING VISIBLE: Digital portfolios give students an opportunity to showcase the evolution of their thinking and understanding and provide you with a resource chock-full of rich information about your students' growth that goes beyond worksheets and multiple-choice questions.

HOW DIGITAL PORTFOLIOS AMPLIFY STUDENT VOICE: These curated demonstrations of learning teach us about your students as individuals, as well as provide your students with a platform through which to find their voice and develop their identity as learners.

HOW DIGITAL PORTFOLIOS ALLOW STUDENTS TO SHARE THEIR WORK: Students publish their digital portfolios online, where their authentic audience becomes their parents, teachers, and peers.

"It sounds a little extreme, but in this day and age, if your work isn't online, it doesn't exist."

—Austin Kleon

4 Cs:
Critical Thinking
Communication
Collaboration
Creativity

ADVANCED:
Curation

SEESAW

WHAT IS SEESAW? Seesaw is a comprehensive, easy-to-use digital portfolio app and website. It is the "Swiss army knife" of creation and reflection apps available.

GREAT BECAUSE … It provides students with a platform to curate their learning while giving their parents insight into their educational growth and progress.

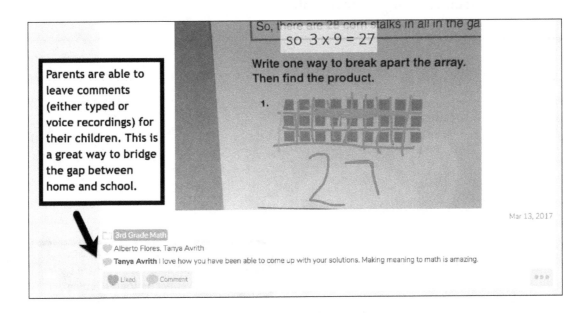

So, there are 28 corn stalks in all in the ga

so 3 x 9 = 27

Write one way to break apart the array. Then find the product.

1.

27

Parents are able to leave comments (either typed or voice recordings) for their children. This is a great way to bridge the gap between home and school.

Mar 13, 2017

3rd Grade Math

Alberto Flores, Tanya Avrith

Tanya Avrith I love how you have been able to come up with your solutions. Making meaning to math is amazing.

Liked   Comment

SET UP IS … EASY. Create your classes, add your students, then provide them with either a QR code or class code so they can enter your class.

Tip: Add a digital portfolio folder for students to add pieces of work they want to include as part of their learning portfolio.

STUDENTS TURN IN WORK BY … selecting the green checkmark in the top-right corner of the screen that turns the students' creations in for the teacher to see.

ALLOWS STUDENTS TO ...

1. take pictures of their "analog" creations where they can add drawings, add text, and record their voice to provide insight on their process;

2. create a video recording within the app;

3. add a written note;

4. add voice, draw on, or add text on a picture that is already saved on the device; insert a picture or video that was created in another app or saved on your desktop or Google Drive;

5. insert a file (i.e., Doc, Slides, Drawing, Sheets) from Google Drive that will be converted as a PDF on Seesaw. Students can add audio annotation or write a text caption.

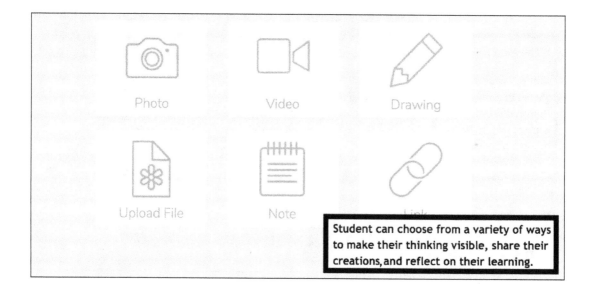

Student can choose from a variety of ways to make their thinking visible, share their creations, and reflect on their learning.

GIVES YOU THE INFORMATION THIS WAY ... It displays your students' work as a class feed in chronological order, similar to a blog.

GOOGLE SITES

WHAT IS GOOGLE SITES? Google Sites is G Suite's webpage-creation platform.

GREAT BECAUSE ... Since Sites is part of G Suite, your students can access their work through their Google account. It allows students to easily insert videos, images, and links. This easy-to-use platform also looks polished, allowing students to create professional looking portfolios to showcase their learning journey.

SET UP IS ... INTERMEDIATE. However, Sites' new drag-and-drop features do make it easy for students to quickly create great-looking websites.

STUDENTS TURN IN WORK BY ... inserting their learning artifacts that are located on their drive into their Google Site. Students can then publish this portfolio site and begin cultivating an authentic audience simply by clicking the "Publish" button and making sure their work is available for public viewing.

GIVES YOU THIS INFORMATION... Sites gives you and your students the option of allowing either a global or restricted audience to view their creations. Sites includes embedded demonstrations of learning and presents students' work in the form of an easy-to-navigate website.

This tool works with other tools, including all G Suite apps, Screencastify, WeVideo, Soundtrap, Canva, and any other tool that uses HTML **coding**.

A GUIDE TO
GETTING STARTED WITH
Digital Portfolios

"Become a
documentarian
of what you do."

—Austin Kleon,
Show Your Work

Making Student Thinking Visible With Digital Portfolios

Digital portfolios provide all of the stakeholders in a student's education—the student themselves, their parents, and us—with rich information about the student's personal learning and growth. That's because these digital tools give learners a place to make their thinking visible, provide them with a voice, and allow them to share (and publish) their creations for an authentic audience. Portfolios also help students curate their learning artifacts, all the while encouraging them to reflect on and think critically about their learning process.

What's more, when done correctly, digital portfolios should replace the need for traditional methods of assessment and evaluation. With portfolios, stakeholders can gain a more critical perspective into a student's understanding and thinking. Ultimately, this gives us insight into their unique path toward academic growth in a way standardized multiple-choice tests cannot. In short, digital portfolios allow us to understand our students as individual learners, each one academically strong and proficient in their own ways.

Where to Begin

Make parents part of the process.

- Start with your students' parents. Including them in this process will help with both the student's and portfolio's success.

- Educate parents on the importance of students developing digital literacy skills, digital footprints, and an understanding of their personal web presence. If you need to skip this step, be sure to send home a notice letting parents know that you're putting their children's work online, or else they may not give you the support you need.

- Open a line of communication between home and school around student learning and sharing student work online. Communicate how this promotes an understanding of digital citizenship and online privacy.

- Educate parents on the importance of creating a personal web presence online. After all, we cannot teach digital citizenship in isolation. Students need to be creating content that they are sharing online to fully understand how to use the tools effectively.

THE THREE TYPES OF
Digital Portfolios

PROCESS SHOWCASE HYBRID

To make student thinking visible, students use this portfolio to document and reflect on their learning process. The process portfolio is geared toward student reflection on learning and gathering feedback from an outside audience to help improve the learning.

- *The student creates.* This part of the learning process is connected to the students' demonstrations (evidence) of learning (e.g., digital books, video productions, podcasts, and collaborative writing pieces) and can be an assessment for, of, or as learning, since, after all, students are learning while creating this type of portfolio.

- *The student reflects.* As your students work on their demonstration of learning for the portfolio, encourage them to take time and reflect on this process. Help them make their thinking visible by providing guiding questions or a structure for curating these reflective artifacts that they will use for explaining their learning.

- *The student receives feedback.* At this point, the student can share work with classmates or a larger audience to gather ideas and/or considerations for making the content better before possibly publishing.

- *The student publishes* (optional). As a final step, the student can pick a platform to publish their work. In most cases, publishing is reserved for the showcase pieces we talk about later. This can be done either with the class, with a tool like Seesaw, or in a more public forum using a blog or website.

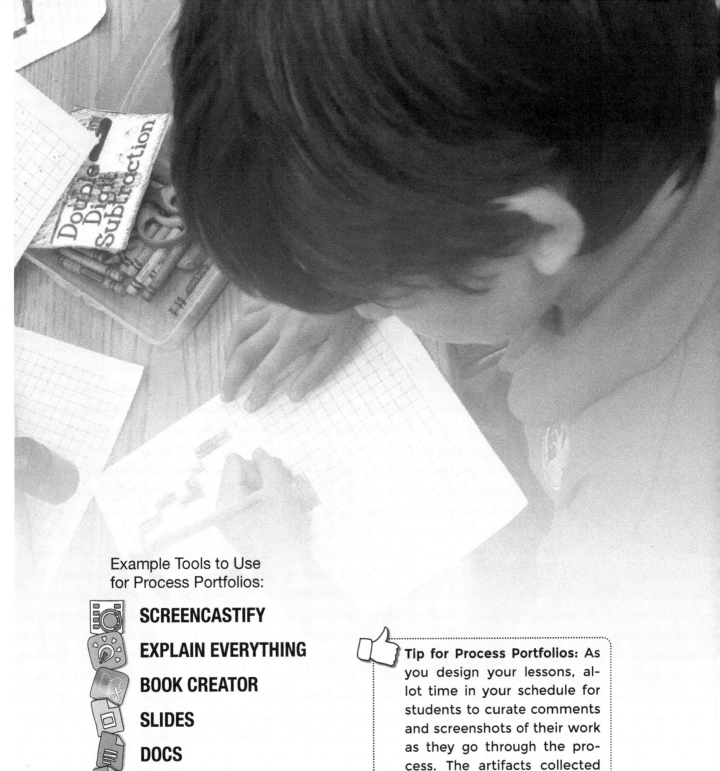

Example Tools to Use
for Process Portfolios:

SCREENCASTIFY

EXPLAIN EVERYTHING

BOOK CREATOR

SLIDES

DOCS

SITES

SEESAW

Tip for Process Portfolios: As you design your lessons, allot time in your schedule for students to curate comments and screenshots of their work as they go through the process. The artifacts collected should demonstrate evidence of growth.

THE THREE TYPES OF
Digital Portfolios

PROCESS **SHOWCASE** HYBRID

Showcase portfolios highlight your students' best work. In a showcase portfolio, students publish the work that is most important to them. Because the student chooses the creation that they believe best demonstrates their learning of a specific target, this portfolio is an assessment *of* learning.

- *The student creates.* At the end of a unit, students will choose an artifact of learning that best demonstrates growth.

- *The student publishes.* As a final step, the student will now pick a platform to publish their showcase work. This can be done either with the class, with a tool like Seesaw, or in a more public forum using a blog or website.

Tip: Make sure student portfolios are created with a simplistic design - something that will catch the eye of the viewer. Too many colors or crazy fonts will not attract an authentic audience.

SOMETHING TO THINK ABOUT:
Blending Analog and Digital

We've been focusing quite a bit on digital artifacts, but sometimes we don't have everything in a digital format. If your students ever find themselves without a digital copy of a creation they'd like to showcase, they need to look no further than a camera. With a quick tap of their smartphone's camera, they can easily create a digital version of an analog creation then take that photograph, throw it on a Site or into a Doc, and begin their reflection process.

Example Tools to Use
for Showcase Portfolios:

GOOGLE SITE

SEESAW

YOUTUBE

GOOGLE SLIDES

Tip for Showcase Portfolios:
Have students share their work
on a social media platform, like
Twitter or Instagram, to build an
audience and connect with experts who might interact with
them to push their thinking and
drive their future learning.

THE THREE TYPES OF
Digital Portfolios

PROCESS   SHOWCASE   **HYBRID**

Hybrid portfolios are a combination of process and showcase portfolios. We can use a hybrid portfolio for an assessment of, for, and as learning. This model allows students to reflect on their learning, choose the pieces they most value and believe best show their growth, and to share those pieces with a larger audience.

Note: This portfolio is similar to the process portfolio but adds in a showcase component as well.

- ***The student creates.*** This part of the learning process is connected to the students' demonstrations of learning (evidence of learning—e.g., digital books, video productions, podcasts, and collaborative writing pieces) and is used as an assessment for, of, or as learning.

- ***The student reflects.*** As your students work on their demonstration of learning for the portfolio, encourage them to take time and reflect on this process. Help them make their thinking visible by providing guiding questions or a structure for curating these reflective artifacts that they will use for explaining their learning.

- ***The student receives feedback.*** If students would like to receive feedback from a larger audience, or even their classmates, the process is simple. Have them digitally capture their work using a camera on a smartphone and/or a tool like Screencastify. While screencasting, students talk through their learning process, then capture and share the final product on a website or on Seesaw, where they can ask for feedback.

- ***The student publishes showcased work.*** Students pick one of their favorite process pieces to showcase and share with the world. There can be several process pieces in the portfolio, but they share only the showcase pieces with the world.

Possible tools to Use
for Hybrid Portfolios:

SCREENCASTIFY

EXPLAIN EVERYTHING

BOOK CREATOR

SLIDES

DOCS

SITES

SEESAW

 TIP FOR HYBRID PORTFOLIOS:
If portfolios are done from year to year, students can expand upon their creations from a previous year, encouraging them to continue working on a project or writing assignment as they improve their skills.

BONUS: TEN WAYS STUDENTS
Can Reach an
Authentic Audience ⋯⋯⋯⋯⋯

1

TWITTER

- Create a Twitter account to connect with classrooms, students, and experts.

- Use hashtags to connect with online communities who share their interests.

- Share blog posts, post YouTube videos they've created, and Tweet <u>BookSnaps.</u>

2

BLOGS

- Blog about their passions, then use Twitter hashtags to promote their posts.

- Use Canva to promote their blog on Twitter, Instagram, and Pinterest.

- Reframe the prompt (see bit.ly/ExampleVideos).

PINTEREST

- Make graphics about their demonstrations of learning on Canva, then promote those images via Pinterest (a search engine), thereby taking people interested in the infographics' subjects to their work.

- The teacher can create classroom boards that link to students' published creations housed on their blogs, allowing their parents to easily find and follow them.

YOUTUBE

- Create vlogs, live content, tutorials, and any other type of video, then place them on their YouTube channel, where they can gain subscribers.

- Curate playlists to attract people to their channel.

FACEBOOK

- Share their creations with their family and friends on a class Facebook page.

- Create a Canva and build an audience by sharing their work.

6 SNAPCHAT

- Create and share fun videos that describe their work.

- Stage a fun reveal of their work, by putting out "coming soon" snaps of their creations.

- Demonstrate their work through videos and pictures.

7 INSTAGRAM

- Share their creations with a larger audience through videos and hashtags.

- Use your class hashtag (for example, #[schoolname]dailywow) to share exciting happenings.

- Stream live events in class with their parents, peers, and followers.

8 CANVA

- Make graphics to attract an audience to the student work or blog.

- Create and print posters with QR codes to post around their school so they can promote their digital work.

> "Tell me, and I will forget. Show me, and I may remember. Involve me, and I will understand."
>
> —Confucius, circa 450BC

9 HASHTAGS

- Find and connect with online communities.

- Host a chat about something they're passionate about or join an already established chat and interact with its participants.

10 SOCIAL MEDIA SCHEDULERS

- Learn how to use social media schedulers like TweetDeck to ensure tweets go out during Twitter's high-traffic times.

Start Here for Tools

In this section, we'll examine the concepts discussed in the Pedagogy section of the book, but with a tool-focused approach—a classroom approach. Think of this "Tools" section as the "What" section and the Pedagogy section as the "Why and How." This section gives you a tool box, explains what you need to consider when choosing a tool, and much more.

THE
TOOLS

WHY GOOGLE?

Within the course of a decade, Google has both changed the face of education in ways few of us could have ever imagined and quickly become one of educators' go-to technology tools. But *why* are Google products—its G Suite—so popular in the classroom? It comes down to a few very simple reasons. Accessibility, sharing, collaboration, and it's all free for schools!

What is a Google Infusion?

A Google infusion is simple: It is a fun way to incorporate some of the great tools available in the Google Ecosystem—Drive, Chrome apps and extensions, and Google Classroom—and partner those with another web- or app-based tool to amplify teaching and learning in your classroom. An example of an infusion might be using Google Classroom to pass out a Flipgrid, or using the Chrome extension Talk and Comment in Google Docs. As you go through the book, you may think of your own "infusions," and we would love to hear about them! Please share them using the hashtag #infusedlearning. We invite you to share your thinking and learning with the world—something that is at the heart of this book.

*** WHAT'S A GOOGLE EXTENSION? ◄ • • • • • • • • •

Small feature-rich applications that live to the right of the Google Omnibox (or address bar), that help personalize your browsing and productivity experience. You get them by going to and searching the Chrome Web Store, which can be found online at chrome.google.com/webstore.

A Quick Look
AT THE GOOGLE ECOSYSTEM

The Google Ecosystem is comprised of all the tools that have been created by Google, and therefore fall under the Google umbrella. For schools, these tools are called the G Suite of Apps and are completely free, promote collaboration, and can be shared in real time between devices.

Google apps do not require an Internet connection. Students' can work offline, and *voilà*, as soon as they are back online their work syncs automatically. G Suite apps have a simple, scaled down design, which allows students to focus on content—not on word art and different shadowing.

This book concentrates on some of the following tools within the Google Ecosystem:

CHROME—Apps and Extensions***
For example: Explain Everything and Talk and Comment

GOOGLE CLASSROOM—This helps the workflow in a classroom by allowing teachers to create, distribute, and grade assignments easily and without the need for a copy machine or printer. Makes passing out, collecting, and grading students' work easy.

GOOGLE DRIVE—Think of Google Drive in this simple way: It is a platform that allows you to store all of your files in the cloud, synchronize those files across many devices, and share them with other users. You can directly upload files from your computer or create new files from within Drive. You can share files and folders so that other users can view, edit, or comment on them. What makes the experience different in the classroom is the focus is on sharing and collaboration.

GOOGLE DOCS—Collectively, the tools that comprise some of Google's most-used tools are referred to as Google Docs. Google Docs, Slides, Sheets, and Forms can be shared and stored on your Google Drive.

Google's
G SUITE

👍 Allows students to collaborate, work efficiently, connect with peers across the globe, and share ideas in real time

👍 Is free for schools

👍 Is a cloud-based platform, meaning students can work on documents on any connected computer wherever they are

👍 Doesn't require an Internet connection—students' work syncs as soon as they are back online

👍 Is integrated into a variety of third-party apps and Chrome extensions, adding functionality to the students' workflow and letting them use these services without ever providing additional information

👍 Saves automatically so students never have to remember to save their work

👍 Has an intentionally simple design, which allows the focus to be on creating content

👍 Makes passing out, collecting, and grading students' work easy

👍 Allows students to publish their work for a large, authentic audience

👍 Has video capabilities

👍 Lets you limit your students' email inter-school communications as needed

Critical Considerations
WHEN CHOOSING A TOOL

How can you determine the best tools to use with your students? We've collected our guiding principles for you to consider.

Is the app easy to use?

Is it easy for students to set up?

Does it give students a place to leave comments?

Is it always free, or are there costs associated with it?

Can students sign into it with their Google account?

Can students use the tool to share their creations with a global audience?

Can students easily download their creations from it onto their desktop or Google Drive?

Can students use the tool to add text, images, voiceovers, and videos to their work?

Is it available on multiple platforms, including iPads, desktops, and Chromebooks?

Is the tool FERPA and COPPA compliant?

Does it help students make their thinking visible, give them a voice, and allow them to share their work?

How easily does it allow parents see their children's work?

WE HAVE CAREFULLY SELECTED 20 TOOLS FOR THIS BOOK. The tools have different purposes that allow students to create artifacts of learning, reflect and curate, connect and share their learning to an authentic audience, and help them learn how to critically consume information.

MEET THE TOOLS

Blogger
BLOGGER.COM

Blogger is a Google-owned blogging platform that you and your students can use to regularly update a learning log, class journal, or website.

Book Creator
BOOKCREATOR.COM

Book Creator is a website and iOS app that allows students to create books, comics, journals, and authentic learning artifacts, which they can then publish online for others to view and read.

Canva
CANVA.COM

Canva is a free online graphic design platform that allows you to quickly create professional, customized graphics. In the company's own words, it's "an amazingly simple graphic design tool."

Classroom
CLASSROOM.GOOGLE.COM

Google Classroom is an online platform for distributing and collecting student work through the Google ecosystem.

DOCS
DOCS.GOOGLE.COM
Google Docs allows multiple students to easily edit, comment on, and view a single document in real time.

Explain Everything
EXPLAINEVERYTHING.COM
Explain Everything is a whiteboard app that lets you draw, create content, import most file formats, record and narrate everything happening on your screen, and export the captured response or video to anywhere.

Flipgrid
FLIPGRID.COM
Flipgrid is a video-response platform using grids where students go to view posted topics, record their responses, and reply to their classmates.

Formative
GOFORMATIVE.COM
Formative is a powerful web-based tool that's perfect for gathering information about student learning. It offers students multiple ways to respond, including the ability to write on their screens. This then allows them to see the process they went through to solve a problem, such as a math equation.

Forms
FORMS.GOOGLE.COM
Google Forms is a G Suite app through which you collect student responses and then display them as graphs and a spreadsheet, creating a quick and easy way to view data.

Padlet
PADLET.COM
Padlet is both a website and a Chrome extension that lets you create a blank digital wall where you can gather student work, answers, or any other type of information that will help inform your teaching and serve as a baseline for upcoming instruction.

MEET THE TOOLS

ReCap App
APP.LETSRECAP.COM

Recap is an app that encourages students to verbalize their thoughts and more deeply reflect on their learning by regularly creating video reflections using provided questions as prompts.

Screencastify
SCREENCASTIFY.COM

Screencastify is a Chrome extension that captures and records all of the screen activity that takes place within a tab, including the audio.

Seesaw
WEB.SEESAW.ME

Seesaw is a comprehensive, easy to use digital portfolio app and website.

Sites
SITES.GOOGLE.COM

Google Sites is a collaborative web page creation platform in the G Suite of products.

Slides
SLIDES.GOOGLE.COM
Google Slides is an online collaborative and visual space that allows students to create and share.

Socrative
SOCRATIVE.COM
Socrative is a website and app that allows you to quickly gather information about your students' learning in the form of closed- and open-ended questions.

Soundtrap
SOUNDTRAP.COM
Soundtrap is a collaborative digital audio workstation that allows you and your students to create sound recordings.

WeVideo
WEVIDEO.COM
WeVideo is a web-based video creation platform.

Talk and Comment
TALKANDCOMMENT.COM
Talk and Comment is a Chrome extension that (once installed) lives on the right or middle side of every website, including Google Docs and Slides. It gives students the ability to leave voice notes in any page with a web address.

YouTube
YOUTUBE.COM
YouTube is a video-hosting website that allows users to upload, view, share, edit, and comment on videos. It is also a powerful search engine and lets students subscribe to your channels.

WHAT THE TOOLS DO

COLLABORATE

Book Creator
Docs
Slides
WeVideo
Soundtrap
Padlet
Sites
Explain Everything

CREATE VIDEOS

WeVideo
Explain Everything
Screencastify
FlipGrid
Recap App
Seesaw
YouTube

PUBLISH

Padlet
Blogger
Seesaw
Sites
Book Creator
Classroom
Docs

Slides
FlipGrid
Recap App
Explain Everything
WeVideo
YouTube
Soundtrap

IMAGE EDITING

Canva
Explain Everything
Slides

CREATE BOOKS/JOURNALS

Book Creator
Docs
Explain Everything
Slides

DIGITAL PORTFOLIOS

Seesaw
Sites
Book Creator

CREATE PRESENTATIONS

Slides
Explain Everything
Canva

CREATE AUDIO FILES

Soundtrap
Book Creator
Seesaw
Talk and Comment
Explain Everything
FlipGrid
Recap

SHOW WHAT YOU KNOW/ FORMATIVE ASSESSMENT

SeeSaw
Socrative
Go Formative
Forms ReCap
Flipgrid

Book Creator
Soundtrap
WeVideo
Screencastify
Blogger

SCREENCAST

Explain Everything
Screencastify
Seesaw

Here are some examples to help you make the best decisions.

Teachers are always looking for ways to use technology to upgrade what's already working in the classroom. This chart will help you decide which tools will best help you integrate technology in your classroom. Use these tips as a starting point and as you create your own Google infusions, be sure to share your ideas on Twitter or Instagram using the #infusedclassroom hashtag.

WERE YOU DOING THIS... **TRY THIS!**

WERE YOU DOING THIS...	TRY THIS!
Make PowerPoint presentations	Edit a video, screencast Slides to explain learning (bit.ly/ExampleVideos), tell stories using Google's My Maps, or create TED Talks.
Complete worksheets, even digital ones	Use an avatar to retell the story, create memes in Google Draw, and gather understandings using **InsertLearning**. (Practice comprehension)
	Make a tutorial for a skill, then place it in a Book Creator book. (Hone skills)
	Create videos showing what words mean or develop synonym journals. (Learn vocabulary)
	Take voice notes using Talk and Comment or create a podcast news story on what happened (bit.ly/ExampleVideos). (Recall)
	Make a "Twitter" board and post facts, statistics, and other relevant information about a concept. (Research)
Build dioramas	Create a virtual world in CoSpaces or Minecraft (bit.ly/ExampleVideos.)
Complete homework packets	Create a family cookbook or blog, play outside with friends, read interest-driven books, have discussions with family members, or start a family-run side business.

Read textbooks	Create **HyperDocs**, make and upload content-specific videos to YouTube, or create books through Book Creator for next year's class.
Take multiple-choice tests and fill out worksheets	Choose the Short Answer Quick Question option in Socrative, populate a short story with open-ended questions in **InsertLearning**, or create video explanations of concepts in a **learning journal** using Book Creator.
Do workbooks	Make interactive notebooks, blogs, or tutorials. This way, students are creating their own learning examples and have them in a "notebook" or blog to refer to a later time when needed.
Take spelling tests	Create **comic vocabulary books** or develop a **word studies** journal, where, instead of memorizing unrelated words, you study words' spelling patterns, roots, prefixes, and other parts, using Book Creator.
Fill in reading logs	Share **BookSnaps** on Snapchat and Instagram.
Partake in round-robin reading	Create **reading fluency journals** in Book Creator.
Design brochures	Create blogs, websites through Google Sites, or **infographics** on Canva.
Create posters	Make a video to explain a project using ThingLink.
Participate in linear notetaking	Sketchnote and participate in collaborative notetaking using Google Docs or Explain Everything.
Follow teacher-created rubrics	Create personalized learning targets.
Take standardized tests	Make demonstrations of learning and curate digital portfolios.
Write book reports	Create movie trailers using WeVideo. Record videos in Seesaw that describe, review, and rate a book. Create a collaborative Amazon-style review website using Google Sites, then add video reviews. You can then link those reviews to a QR code that you print and attach to hard-copy versions of a book for people to scan and watch your reviews. Write and record a movie pitch for the book to present to a Hollywood producer using Screencastify. Collect items in a book box that represent key objects in the story, then either write or verbalize an explanation for each object using Screencastify or your cell phone.

Rethinking Teaching
TRADITIONAL VS. TRANSFORMATIONAL

Here are some examples to help you make the best decisions.

If our students are to succeed in this twenty-first-century world, it's important that we transition from traditional, teacher-led educational practices to ones that effectively incorporate technology and focus on our students and their need for **differentiated** learning. We know this can initially be difficult to envision, so here are just a few ways you could incorporate transformational teaching into your classroom.

TRADITIONAL TEACHING ◄··············►	TRANSFORMATIONAL TEACHING
Teaching is standardized.	Teaching is personalized.
The teacher is in control of the classroom.	Students have a voice in the direction the class takes (**student agency**).
The teacher is the keeper of information.	The students and teachers work together to discover information.
Students' compliance is dependent upon the threat of punishment for non-adherence.	Students take initiative for their learning and are trusted to be on- and off-task.
Information is static and either gleaned from textbooks or a prescribed curriculum.	Information comes from a variety of resources, including social learning networks, validated online sources, and curated experts.
Worksheets are made months in advance and curriculum is stored in a binder.	Lessons are dynamic and led by students' questions, prior knowledge, curiosities, and needs.
Subjects are divided and compartmentalized.	Subjects overlap and connections are drawn.

TRADITIONAL TEACHING ◄•••••••••••►	TRANSFORMATIONAL TEACHING
The curriculum is delivered in parts and sections, and the product is graded.	The curriculum focuses on the process, with the teacher assessing students' individual growth.
Students sit in rows of desks with the teacher in the front of the room.	The classroom is a flexible learning environment designed with the students' needs in mind.
Educators use prescribed lesson plans.	Students are involved in the process of developing their learning targets.
Assessments of knowledge involve standardized testing and multiple-choice tests.	Students create digital portfolios and demonstrations of learning.
Teachers and parents are the sole audience for students' work.	The world is the audience for students' creations.
Students complete homework.	Students work on **20% Time** projects.

Experimenting with technology can be a fun, empowering experience for both us and our students alike. By effectively integrating constructivism and connectivism into our classrooms, we can design the kind of twenty-first-century learning landscape conducive to this experimentation while also preparing our students for the future.

And remember: The best lessons never focus on the tools or the technology we use; rather, they focus on student learning.

Two learning theories that we discuss in the "Start with Pedagogy" section explain how our twenty-first-century learners need to learn. Based on these learning theories, we have outlined some examples of how the TOOLS of technology can be used to make our classrooms centers of curiosity and learning.

Dive into Inquiry

Amplify Learning and Empower Student Voice

By Trevor MacKenzie

Dive into Inquiry beautifully marries the voice and choice of inquiry with the structure and support required to optimize learning. With *Dive into Inquiry* you'll gain an understanding of how to best support your learners as they shift from a traditional learning model into the inquiry classroom where student agency is fostered and celebrated each and every day.

Inquiry Mindset

Nurturing the Dreams, Wonders, and Curiosities of Our Youngest Learners

By Trevor MacKenzie and Rebecca Bathurst-Hunt

Inquiry Mindset offers a highly accessible journey through inquiry in the younger years. Learn how to empower your students, increase engagement, and accelerate learning by harnessing the power of curiosity. With practical examples and a step-by-step guide to inquiry, Trevor MacKenzie and Rebecca Bathurst-Hunt make inquiry-based learning simple.

Sketchnotes for Educators

100 Inspiring Illustrations for Lifelong Learners

By Sylvia Duckworth

Sylvia Duckworth is a Canadian teacher whose sketchnotes have taken social media by storm. Her drawings provide clarity and provoke dialogue on many topics related to education. This book contains 100 of her most popular sketchnotes with links to the original downloads that can be used in class or shared with colleagues. Interspersed throughout the book are Sylvia's reflections on each drawing and what motivated her to create them, in addition to commentary from other educators who inspired the sketchnotes.

How to Sketchnote

A Step-by-Step Manual for Teachers and Students

By Sylvia Duckworth

Educator and internationally known sketchnoter Sylvia Duckworth makes ideas memorable and shareable with her simple yet powerful drawings. In *How to Sketchnote*, she explains how you can use sketchnoting in the classroom and that you don't have to be an artist to discover the benefits of doodling!

Bring meaningful and high energy PD
TO YOUR SCHOOL, DISTRICT OR EVENT.

The Infused Classroom Workshops are designed with an emphasis on purposeful technology integration.

It is always customized to fit the needs of your school or district, and promises to be one of the best, most hands-on PD experiences around.

In this **hands-on and high energy** masterclass, we will look at some of the most popular and simple tools that can be used to amplify teaching and learning in the classroom. While tools are important, understanding the pedagogical ways we can use them to transform teaching is even more critical, and this **masterclass will lay out a path for allowing teachers and students to make meaning of content.** By the end of the day, educators will have learned how to better use technology to support and amplify the learning experiences in their classrooms.

This masterclass will be built around the **learning framework that helps educators make student thinking and learning visible,** allows teachers to hear from every student and gives students a way to meaningfully share their work.

The workshop will include a look at:

- Formative Assessment Ideas
- Differentiated Instruction Techniques
- Demonstrations of Learning
- Reflection Ideas

To inquire about speaking engagements,
fill out the form: **bit.ly/InfusedPD**

Email: **info@elevatebooks.edu**

ABOUT THE AUTHORS

Holly Clark is an education strategist from San Diego, California. She is a Google Certified Innovator, National Board Certified Teacher, and holds an MA in Technology in Education from Teachers College, Columbia University. She has been working with technology integration and 1:1 environments since the year 2000. Presently she consults with schools internationally on building both the culture and strategy to support and inspire innovative teaching, including meaningful technology integration and design thinking protocols.

Holly has taught in both independent and public schools and is the co-founder of #CaEdChat. She authors a popular education blog: hollyclark.org and gives keynotes to audiences worldwide.

Connect with Holly

Blog: hollyclark.org

Twitter @HollyClarkEdu

Email: holly@hollyclark.org

Tanya Avrith is a teacher and pedagogical consultant living in southern Florida. She is a Google Certified Innovator and an Apple Distinguished Educator, and holds an MA in Educational Technology. Tanya has taught at the elementary, middle, and high school levels and has consulted with schools to plan and execute large-scale deployments and professional-development plans for digital citizenship and iPad and Chromebook initiatives.

She previously served as the lead educational and digital citizenship teacher at the Lester B. Pearson School Board in Montreal, Canada, and currently teaches Personal Branding and Digital Communication to high school students at North Broward Prep in Coconut Creek, Florida.

Connect with Tanya

Twitter @TanyaAvrith

Website: tanyaavrith.com

Email: tanya@tanyaavrith.com